The Old Mass and the New

MARC AILLET, C.S.M.

The Old Mass and the New:

Explaining the Motu Proprio *Summorum Pontificum* of Pope Benedict XVI

TRANSLATED BY HENRY TAYLOR

IGNATIUS PRESS   SAN FRANCISCO

Original French edition:
Un évènement liturgique
© 2007 by éditions Tempora, Perpignan

Motu Proprio *Summorum Pontificum*
© Libreria Editrice Vaticana

Cover inset: Detail from the retable of the chapel of
St. Mary's College, Oscott, by A.W.N. Pugin.
Photograph by Lawrence Lew, O.P.

Background image: "Agnus Dei", mid seventeenth-century.
Etching by Wenceslaus Holler (1607–1677).

Cover design by John Herreid

© 2010 Ignatius Press, San Francisco
ISBN 978-1-58617-362-3
Library of Congress Control Number 2010927113
Printed in the United States of America ∞

CONTENTS

FOREWORD

In receiving the motu proprio *Summorum Pontificum Cura*, the Church is encouraged to understand what is at stake here.

This motu proprio does not amount to a mere enticement of the Priestly Fraternity of Saint Pius X. The perspective is broader. It is part of a long-evident desire by Joseph Ratzinger to promote the organic development of the teaching and the liturgy of the Church.

Right after his election, Benedict XVI had specified that one of the main priorities of his pontificate would be "to put the Second Vatican Council into practice, following . . . in faithful continuity with the two-thousand-year tradition of the Church". In his historic address of December 22, 2005, the Sovereign Pontiff had defended the importance of a correct interpretation of Vatican II, rejecting a "hermeneutic of discontinuity and rupture". By contrast, he proposed a hermeneutic of continuity and reform, as a "synthesis of fidelity and dynamic" that could alone bear fruit. The Pope has taken a position entirely consistent with that of his predecessor, John XXIII, who in his speech opening the Council, on October 11, 1962, declared, "It is necessary that this certain and immutable doctrine, which must be faithfully respected, should be studied thoroughly and presented in a way that corresponds to the needs of our times."

The motu proprio is to be seen against the horizon of the plan for a *reform of the reform*, that is to say, the rediscovery of *the spirit of the liturgy* and the progressive resacralization of worship, particularly of the *ordinary rite*.[1] Hence this affirmation, of capital significance: "A renewal of liturgical awareness, a liturgical reconciliation that again recognizes the unity of the history of the liturgy and that understands Vatican II, not as a breach, but as a stage of development: these things are urgently needed for the life of the Church. I am convinced that the crisis in the Church that we are experiencing today is to a large extent due to the disintegration of the liturgy. . . . This is why we need a new Liturgical Movement, which will call to life the real heritage of the Second Vatican Council."[2]

This motu proprio is by no means a step backward. The gesture of reconciliation it expresses calls with prophetic voice for a *liturgical renewal,* based on an increased theological and spiritual appreciation of the principles of the liturgical reform of Vatican II.

Supported by and linked to documents of the Church's Magisterium, Father Marc Aillet, a member of the Community of Saint Martin and Vicar General of the diocese of Fréjus-Toulon, sketches the essential outlines of that renewal, its relevance and timeliness.

This book is a valuable contribution toward continuing that effort of renewal desired by Pius X, initiated by Pius XII, and developed by the Council's constitution *Sacrosanctum Concilium,* an effort that it is more than ever advisable to reexamine and reappropriate. This motu proprio certainly is a *liturgical event.*

+ Most Rev. Dominique Rey
Bishop of the diocese of Fréjus-Toulon

---

[1] Cf. Benedict XVI, apostolic exhortation *Sacramentum Caritatis.*

[2] Joseph Ratzinger, *Milestones: Memoirs 1927–1977,* trans. Erasmo Leiva-Merikakis (San Francisco: Ignatius Press, 1998), 148–49.

PREFACE

Benedict XVI has dared to do it. Announced as forthcoming for months, awaited by some with frantic impatience, dreaded by others with some anxiety, the motu proprio was finally published on July 7, 2007, with the title of *Summorum Pontificum*. It was accompanied by a personal letter from the Pope to the bishops, to explain the reasons for his decision.[1]

The press, whether ill-informed or ill-intentioned, denounced the victory of traditionalist pressure groups, considerably overestimating their influence on the Pope, who is said to be "conservative". It said nothing, on the other hand, about the pressure that may have been brought to bear on him to try to modify his decision: people had even brandished the politico-religious specter of the encouragement that would supposedly be given to the extreme right, since the sociological context of our country was so far beyond the insight of the Roman Curia.[2] In any case, it was the first time in thirty years that some fear for the authority of the bishops where liturgy was concerned[3] and that some objected to the risk of "subjectivism" in the way it was celebrated. And then it was necessary to reassure the directors

[1] See the appendices at the end of the book.

[2] The oppositions between left and right, "progressives" and "fundamentalists", are part of a past in which the younger generations decidedly no longer recognize themselves as having a place.

[3] Contrary to all expectations, this fear was expressed by circles among whom we had not been used to finding such deference toward episcopal authority.

of the reform, whose goodwill can rightly be acknowledged but who had been sent to work with so little liturgical formation.

The Pope felt quite free to take his time. After "much reflection [and] numerous consultations" and not without having "invoked the Holy Spirit and trusting in the help of God", he made his decision: the old and new Missals are called to coexist in the Church, the first as the extraordinary form, and the second as the ordinary form, of the single Roman rite. People got upset, and certain bishops even gave warm expression to their "perplexity". Yet after a few weeks the excitement subsided, and everyone agreed to respect a desire for communion that cannot be rejected. In any case, for the moment, no one has been inundated with requests.

For some, the motu proprio is a *victory*; for others, a *nonevent*. There is no doubt it is in the first place a gesture toward "coming to an interior reconciliation in the heart of the Church", made in the direction of some of the faithful who have great difficulty in living their communion in practice. Might not this kind of disciplinary measure, which assuredly has a highly symbolic value, nonetheless have the salutary effect of drawing the attention of both pastors and faithful toward taking more trouble about the dignity and the sacral nature of liturgical celebration? Might not this motu proprio quite simply have the purpose of relaunching the *liturgical movement*, which, as we certainly have to admit, had become somewhat bogged down in the marshy meanderings of unbridled creativity and arbitrary distortions? That is the view I shall take in these pages.

The fact is that, if the immediate subject of the *Summorum Pontificum* certainly is "the use of the Roman liturgy prior to the reform of 1970", it clearly has far wider aims in view and constitutes an invitation to take up again the spirit of the liturgy that the liturgical movement had helped to rediscover in so promising a way. My intention here, then, is not to praise the earlier Missal, but rather to attribute full value to the principles of liturgical reform and to highlight the theological and spiritual treasures of the new Missal.

In the first chapter, we will give a succinct analysis of the motu proprio and the letter accompanying it, linking this with the recent recommendations of the Magisterium concerning the dignity of the liturgy. We will show in the second chapter how this motu proprio is calling for a new *liturgical movement*, to help us out of what it is certainly appropriate to call a *crisis for the liturgy*. Finally, in the third chapter, we will demonstrate the continuity between the two Missals by studying the concept of *active participation* unfolded in the Second Vatican Council's constitution *Sacrosanctum Concilium* on the sacred liturgy. It goes without saying that our study will be undertaken in the light of a careful reading of the post-synodal apostolic exhortation *Sacramentum Caritatis*, issued by Benedict XVI just a few months before the motu proprio.

INTRODUCTION
A Personal Testimony

It is as a member of the Community of Saint Martin since its founding thirty years ago,[1] and as Vicar General of the Diocese of Fréjus-Toulon since 2002, that I should like to make my modest contribution to the task of renewing the liturgy that was started by the Second Vatican Council and put back on the agenda by the recent motu proprio *Summorum Pontificum*. This I will do less as a specialist than as someone who celebrates the liturgy and as a pastor, inasmuch as the liturgy has an eminently pastoral dimension.

What distinguishes the Community of Saint Martin in the French liturgical landscape is its choice, as the preferred form of its liturgical life, of the so-called *Ordo Missae* of Paul VI, celebrated in Latin with Gregorian chant. The book of customs of the Community of Saint Martin lays down that, while giving due attention to any possible adaptations that might be required by educational or pastoral considerations, "we are committed to liturgical celebration in Latin and to Gregorian chant." Nonetheless, we are committed to encouraging and facilitating as much as possible the participation of the faithful.

---

[1] I should make clear that in these candid remarks I make no claim to be speaking on behalf of the Community of Saint Martin as such, even if I am fully committed to its liturgical grace.

Monsignor Jean-François Guérin, the founder of the Community of Saint Martin, had been an oblate of the Benedictine Abbey of Fontgombault[2] since his ordination in 1955; his love for the liturgy had grown stronger and his *ars celebrandi* had acquired depth—he was able to hand these on to us with passionate enthusiasm. In 1970 he had changed from the Missal of Saint Pius V to that of Paul VI, making his assent to the renewed form of the liturgy the expression of his *sensus Ecclesiae*: thus, we were invited to receive from today's Church—"on condition that it should be in a spirit of reform and not of rupture", to use the words of Benedict XVI's lecture on the hermeneutics of the Second Vatican Council, delivered to the Roman curia on December 22, 2005—all the good things we needed in order to grow in our sense of the Church. As he loved to say, during those years of the seventies, which saw great tensions within the French Church from which he had suffered a great deal: "Nothing of our legitimate affection for tradition, for the liturgy, for Holy Scripture, or for the Virgin Mary can justify deliberately setting ourselves outside the Church." In connecting us with the centuries-old, uninterrupted tradition of the liturgy of the Latin Church, Latin and Gregorian chant have certainly been the special instruments of our formation in Christian and priestly life, making the liturgy

---

[2] The Benedictine Abbey of Fontgombault is widely known in France as a center where the "old Mass" of Pius V/John XXIII continues to be celebrated in Latin, with Gregorian chant (and similarly for the monastic offices), while the abbey remains completely within the obedience of Rome. In July 2001 it was the setting for an important conference, chaired by Joseph Ratzinger and aimed at healing the wounds of the "new Mass—old Mass" opposition. English translation of the proceedings: *Looking Again at the Question of the Liturgy with Cardinal Ratzinger* (Farnborough: Saint Michael's Abbey Press, 2003).—TRANS.

the primary structural element of that formation. I can bear witness that the liturgy, thus experienced and lived during seminary years and in the first years of pastoral ministry, shaped my baptismal and priestly existence. Was that not what Mother Geneviève Gallois was suggesting, in her *Life of Little Placidus*, when she had Jesus saying to Saint Benedict's young novice, in the style of a proverb, "The liturgy means spending your life passing into my life", and prompting little Placidus in turn to this maxim, "Singing His life so as to live my song."[3]

As a priest who has exercised various ministries within the diocese of Fréjus-Toulon (youth chaplain, lecturer at the diocesan seminary, and parish priest), I have experienced the liturgy, the *source* and *summit of the life of the Church*, as the one setting par excellence for the formation of the faithful in the Christian life; at one and the same time it educates them in the sense of faith, by the revelation of the Mystery of which the liturgy must be the eloquent symbol, and in the sense of the Church, which remains the proper subject of the liturgy. As we can read in the constitution *Sacrosanctum Concilium*: "Every liturgical celebration, because it is an action of Christ the priest and of His Body which is the Church, is a sacred action surpassing all others; no other action of the Church can equal its efficacy by the same title and to the same degree" (§7).

---

[3] As the fruit of its community and pastoral experience of the Gregorian liturgy and as a contribution to the liturgical renewal initiated by the Second Vatican Council, the Community of Saint Martin is currently working toward the publication of a Latin-French version of the *Gregorian Hours*, making it possible, for anyone who wishes to do so, to sing the Liturgy of the Hours in Gregorian chant. This is being done with the approval of the Congregation for Divine Worship (in its decree of July 9, 2004) and with the expert collaboration of the Abbey of Solesmes.

As Vicar General, I have been led to work with my bishop, the Most Rev. Dominique Rey, in setting up in 2005 a personal parish for the so-called Tridentine liturgy, following the motu proprio *Ecclesia Dei Adflicta*. This was a different way of demonstrating my *sensus Ecclesiae*, since Pope John Paul II was asking bishops to "a wide and generous application" of the opportunity offered to the faithful who requested it of participating in the liturgy according to the books in use in 1962. As Ordinary, I have thus been led to celebrate the so-called Mass of Saint Pius V—something for which I had not been prepared in my community—and I have been able to appreciate the fundamental continuity between the two Missals. I am even convinced that it is possible to celebrate the Mass according to either of the two Missals in the spirit of the constitution *Sacrosanctum Concilium*, as Pope John Paul II had already suggested.

I

A MOTU PROPRIO THAT IS
PART OF A CONTINUITY

The Holy Father Benedict XVI, following "much reflection, numerous consultations and prayer" has finally published an apostolic letter in the form of a motu proprio on the use of the Roman liturgy prior to the reform of 1970. The long-awaited measures foresee a certain *easing of restrictions* on the *Ordo Missae* known as that of Saint Pius V in its most recent edition, the one published by Pope John XXIII in 1962, referred to from now on as the *Missal of Blessed John XXIII*.

1. The Provisions of the Motu Proprio

It is not a matter of *backtracking* and thus attenuating the authority of the Second Vatican Council, or, in particular, of casting doubt upon the liturgical reform that was decided there, as Benedict XVI is careful to make clear in his letter to bishops on the occasion of the publication of his motu proprio. Thus he declares that there is an essential distinction between the *forma ordinaria* of the *lex orandi*, which remains the Missal promulgated by Pope Paul VI in 1970, and its *forma extraordinaria* constituted by the Missal existing before the Council, which has never been abrogated. These two forms do not establish two rites; rather they are two usages of one and the same Roman rite (art. 1).

Thus the aim of the motu proprio is not to advocate either a general return to the old Missal or the use of the two Missals indiscriminately in the ordinary life of our ecclesial communities. In essence, then, this motu proprio makes no change in the present situation, despite the proclamations of its detractors, whom Benedict XVI discreetly calls to order in his letter: "News reports and judgments made without sufficient information have created no little confusion . . . about a plan whose contents were in reality unknown." Meaning to be reassuring, if necessary, the Holy Father explains that in fact "the new Missal will certainly remain the ordinary Form of the Roman Rite, not only on account of the juridical norms, but also because of the actual situation of the communities of the faithful."

The change made in comparison with the indult of 1984, which Pope John Paul II asked the bishops to apply in a "wide and generous" way in his motu proprio *Ecclesia Dei Adflicta* in 1988, is the establishment of "specific norms for the possible use of the earlier Missal". These norms concern any priest of the Latin rite saying private Mass, known as *sine populo*, who will from now on be able to use without authorization either one of the two forms of the Roman rite (art. 2), even in the presence of faithful who may wish of their own free will to join in (art. 4). The norms provide especially that the parish priest may himself accept a request made in his parish by "a stable group of faithful who adhere to the earlier liturgical tradition" (art. 5 §1). This authorization is thus no longer subject to an indult given by the bishop, who nonetheless retains his role as "moderator of the liturgical life of his diocese", called to ensure that the liturgical norms are respected for either form of the Roman rite, having in view solely the welfare of souls and the unity of the flock, and urged to exercise his pastoral care over all the faithful who are committed to his charge, without exception, referring to §22 of the constitution *Sacrosanctum Concilium*. At the end of his accompanying letter to the bishops, Benedict XVI affirms that "Nothing is taken away, then, from the authority of the Bishop, whose role remains that of being watchful that all is done in peace and serenity."

The motu proprio even specifies that if the faithful who legitimately request this do not obtain what they are asking from the pastor, they will then inform the diocesan bishop, who is "strongly requested to satisfy their wishes". In case of a dispute or obstacle, the matter should ultimately be referred to the Pontifical Commission *Ecclesia Dei* (arts. 7 and 8).

The motu proprio further allows for this opportunity to be extended to the other sacraments and to funerals even for the clergy to use the Roman Breviary promulgated by Blessed John XXIII (art. 9).

Finally, "if he feels it appropriate", the bishop may erect a personal parish in his diocese for celebrations in accordance with the ancient form of the Roman rite (art. 10).

2. The Reasons for the Motu Proprio

It is from a remarkably lofty viewpoint and with a genuine pastoral concern and pedagogical rigor that Pope Benedict takes care to explain to the bishops the reasons for his decision.

a. A liturgical formation wounded by a certain implementation of the reform

The first reason is that many people remain strongly attached to this usage of the Roman rite, and not merely for the psychological or sociological motives that are generally advanced in order to discredit their *petitio* a priori, even though the Holy Father does know "that there have been exaggerations and at times social aspects unduly linked to the attitude of the faithful attached to the ancient Latin liturgical tradition".

Benedict XVI even emphasizes that where it was expected that this request would come exclusively from elderly believers, "it has clearly been demonstrated that the young persons too have discovered this liturgical form, felt its attraction and found in it a form of encounter with the Mystery of the Most Holy Eucharist particularly suited to them." It would in fact be difficult to underestimate the relatively low average age of traditionalist congregations.

Thus, the Holy Father is persuaded that in countries like France, where the "liturgical movement had provided many people with a notable liturgical formation and a deep personal familiarity with the earlier Form of the Liturgical celebration", the attachment to the earlier Missal was well-founded and knowledgeable. This attachment found a further justification in the *arbitrary deformations* that accompanied the reform, which was nonetheless for its own part entirely consistent with the liturgical movement that had in many cases preceded it. With great honesty and clear-sightedness, the Holy Father does in fact write, "the new Missal . . . actually was understood as authorizing or even requiring creativity, which frequently led to deformations of the liturgy which were hard to bear. I am speaking from experience, since I too lived through that period with all its hopes and confusion. And I have seen how arbitrary deformations of the liturgy caused deep pain to individuals totally rooted in the faith of the Church."

b. *A mutual enrichment of the two Missals*

So the Holy Father does not believe that these new arrangements can "lead to disarray or even divisions within parish
communities", as had been protested to him by way of objection. And in charity, with a nice delicacy, he alludes to
the disarray and divisions that have indeed resulted in the
life of the Church through the numerous fantasies that have
been tolerated for the last forty years in implementing the
liturgical reform and that have hidden from many "the spiritual richness and the theological depth" of the new Missal.
To counter the risk of division, he even suggests that one
should insist, rather, on faithfulness to the liturgical norms:
"the most sure guarantee that the Missal of Paul VI can unite
parish communities and be loved by them consists in its being celebrated with great reverence and in harmony with the
liturgical directives."

He even ventures to believe that "the two Forms of the
usage of the Roman Rite can be mutually enriching". In particular, the *extraordinary form* will lead people, in celebrations
of the Mass according to the Missal of Paul VI, to demonstrate "more powerfully than has been the case hitherto the
sacrality which attracts many people to the former usage".

c. *An undertaking of reconciliation within the Church*

Lastly, in explaining the *positive reason* that induced him to
make these arrangements, the Holy Father offers us a fine
example of pastoral governance. For him, this is a matter
of "coming to an interior reconciliation in the heart of the
Church". And he suggests to bishops an *examination of conscience* similar to the one Pope John Paul II proposed as a

preparation for the Great Jubilee of the year 2000:[1] "Looking back over the past, to the divisions which in the course of
the centuries have rent the Body of Christ, one continually
has the impression that, at critical moments when divisions
were coming about, not enough was done by the Church's
leaders to maintain or regain reconciliation and unity. One
has the impression that omissions on the part of the Church
have had their share of blame for the fact that the divisions
were able to harden." Everything possible should therefore
be done to allow everyone to remain in unity or to regain it.
It is said very tactfully, yet this is nonetheless an invitation
to the Church's leaders to a true *mea culpa.*

3. Earlier Recommendations

The arbitrary deformation denounced by Benedict XVI in
his motu proprio and which he sees as the reason why some
of the faithful have gone back to the earlier Roman Missal,
were stressed time and again by Pope John Paul II. But were
these assertions sufficiently taken into account?

John Paul II concluded the introduction to his fine encyclical *Ecclesia de Eucharistia* with these words: "It is my
hope that the present Encyclical Letter will effectively help
to banish the dark clouds of unacceptable doctrine and practice, so that the Eucharist will continue to shine forth in all
its radiant mystery" (§ 10).

At the end of the chapter devoted to "The Dignity of the
Eucharistic Celebration", he writes, "It must be lamented

---

[1] *Tertio Millennio Adveniente,* § 36: "An examination of conscience must
also consider the *reception given to the Council,* this great gift of the Spirit to
the Church at the end of the second millennium. . . . Is the liturgy lived as
the 'origin and summit' of ecclesial life, in accordance with the teaching of
Sacrosanctum Concilium?"

that, especially in the years following the post-conciliar liturgical reform, as a result of a misguided sense of creativity and adaptation, there have been a number of *abuses* which have been a source of suffering for many" (§ 52). Benedict XVI is saying nothing different in his letter to the bishops. And John Paul II felt it his duty "to appeal urgently that the liturgical norms for the celebration of the Eucharist be observed with great fidelity", the expression for both priest and community that "quietly but eloquently demonstrate(s) their love for the Church". This is the very reason why the Pope asked the competent dicasteries of the Roman Curia "to prepare a more specific document, including prescriptions of a juridical nature, on this very important subject."[2]

In the post-synodal apostolic exhortation *Ecclesia in Europa*, John Paul II once again went over the need for rediscovering the liturgy, but this time with the psychological weight of authority given him by the unanimity of the college of bishops represented at the Synod. "Certain signs", he says, "point to a weakening in the sense of mystery in the very liturgical celebrations which should be fostering that sense. It is, therefore, *urgent that the authentic sense of the liturgy be revived in the Church*" (§ 70). And he adds, "Although in the period following the Second Vatican Ecumenical Council real progress has been made towards experiencing the authentic meaning of the liturgy, much remains to be done. . . . True *renewal*, far from depending on arbitrary actions, consists of constantly developing an awareness of the sense of mystery" (§ 72).

---

[2] The Congregation for Divine Worship and the Discipline of the Sacraments did indeed publish, on March 25, 2004, the instruction *Redemptionis Sacramentum*, on certain things to be observed or to be avoided regarding the Most Holy Eucharist.

4. The Positions of Joseph Cardinal Ratzinger

The reasons Pope Benedict XVI raises in his motu proprio had already been advanced several times by the man who was then simply Joseph Cardinal Ratzinger, Prefect of the Congregation for the Doctrine of the Faith.

On October 24, 1998, on the occasion of the tenth anniversary of the motu proprio *Ecclesia Dei*, he did in fact deliver an important speech in which he was already refuting what he called the two main reasons for opposition to an attachment to the earlier forms of the liturgy: "the two reasons most often heard are a lack of obedience to the Council, which wanted to have the liturgical books reformed, and the break in unity that must necessarily follow if different liturgical forms are left in use". It seemed to him relatively easy to refute these objections.

First, it was not the Council itself that reformed the liturgical books; it simply ordered their revision, setting out some fundamental rules, which were also to be respected for celebrating according to the old Missal: "That is why it is important to observe the essential criteria of the Constitution on the Liturgy . . . also when one celebrates according to the old Missal!"

Next, he opposes as false the suggestion that there is any risk of a break in unity:

> The freedom given to creativity by the new order of Mass is often stretched too far; the difference between the liturgy according to the new books, how it is actually practiced and celebrated in various places, is often greater than that between the old liturgy and the new, when they are both celebrated in accordance with the prescribed liturgical books.

An average Christian, without any special liturgical formation, would find it difficult to distinguish between a Mass
sung in Latin according to the old Missal and a Mass sung
in Latin according to the new Missal; on the other hand,
the difference between a Mass celebrated according to the
Missal of Paul VI and the actual forms and celebrations in
the vernacular with all the freedom and creativity possible
—that difference can be enormous.

Cardinal Ratzinger spoke many times in favor of a return
to a sense of the sacred and of mystery in the celebration
according to the new Missal:

> Many reasons have induced people to seek refuge in the old
> liturgy. One of the main and most important is that they
> perceive that the dignity of the sacred is better preserved
> there. After the Council, there were many who quite delib-
> erately laid the foundations for a program of *desacralization*,
> explaining that the New Testament had abolished the cult
> of the Temple: the veil that was torn from top to bottom
> signified—according to them—the end of the sacred. . . .
> Using reasoning like this, they gave up sacred vestments,
> despoiled churches, and reduced the liturgy to the language
> and the gestures of everyday life.[3]

Indeed, we do have to note that, whatever the at times ideological or political presuppositions motivating those who
have reacted against what they call a *break with tradition*
brought about by implementing the liturgical reform, that
reaction does include a profession of faith in the objective
nature of the rite that appears in opposition to the all too
frequently subjective relationship to the liturgy that governs
many liturgical celebrations. Thus it seems to me that if this

---

[3] Address of July 13, 1988, to the Chilean Bishops' Conference.

motu proprio—even at the risk of calling into question certain *acquired rights* (acquired through disobedience)—could correct our subjective ways of celebrating, that would be an excellent thing.

II

TOWARD A NEW
"LITURGICAL MOVEMENT"

The reactions of anxiety from this or that priest or lay liturgical leader to the publication of the motu proprio should not be surprising: their comments reveal a lack of liturgical formation and of theological sense, which is in any case not always their fault. The liturgical reform has been so reduced to its exterior and technical aspects that very often, in the name of ideological presuppositions we cannot refrain from mentioning, the liturgy has been turned into material that is at the disposition of the celebrant and/or liturgical team. That being the case, how can the Holy Father's decision be understood as anything but an *intransigence* or *retreat*, especially since the implementation of the reform was frequently accompanied by a *diabolizing* of the earlier liturgy, which was caricatured by certain pastors, and since grave injustice has even been done to this or that priest or group of the faithful who, in the name of a deep liturgical formation, quite simply refused to do anything, while filially accepting the Second Vatican Council and the new Missal.[1]

For all that, this is not a matter of discouraging those who have been active in implementing the liturgical reform, but,

---

[1] I am speaking from experience, as the Community of Saint Martin came into being in just such an ecclesial context thirty years ago and was committed from the start to the 1970 Missal!

on the contrary, of encouraging them to make renewed efforts to receive the true heritage of Vatican II and, in particular, of prompting them to acquire a more profound liturgical formation and a greater familiarity with "the spiritual richness and the theological depth of the new Missal".

1. A Hermeneutic of the Reform

It cannot be noted often enough that the key to understanding the motu proprio lies in one of the last paragraphs of Benedict XVI's letter to the bishops: "There is no contradiction between the two editions of the Roman Missal. In the history of the liturgy there is growth and progress, but no rupture. What earlier generations held as sacred remains sacred and great for us too, and it cannot be all of a sudden entirely forbidden or even considered harmful. It behooves all of us to preserve the riches which have developed in the Church's faith and prayer and give them their proper place." This is the crux of the question, and that goes for those who claim, on the basis of a dubious theology, that the 1970 Missal broke with tradition just as much as for those who naïvely think that the theological paradigms, and thus the concept of liturgy, have been changed.

The Pope's intentions go far beyond making a gesture toward traditionalist Catholics—and even in that sense, it already has much pastoral significance.[2] Its aim is to reconcile Catholics with their centuries-old heritage: a concern

---

[2] One objection to these new arrangements has been the relatively limited number of the faithful attached to the old form of the liturgy, which the editorial writer of *La Croix* has even compared—not without a certain degree of contempt—to the "billion Catholics" to be counted throughout the world, as if, by the way, we in France could congratulate ourselves on the great and growing number of practicing faithful using the new Missal. Nonetheless,

not merely for *synchronic communion*, but also for *diachronic communion*. A logic of rupture has inspired many theologians and pastors since the Second Vatican Council, part of a *mentality of disjuncture* that in our own country rose to a paroxysm during the French Revolution and was expressed in our own time in May 1968. Above and beyond the *lex orandi* there is the *lex credendi*, of which the liturgy is the privileged expression. No one could deny that since the Second Vatican Council, confusion has reigned in the realm of theology and then be surprised at the current liturgical abuses. Allow me at this point to refer to the very pertinent analysis of Father Michel Gitton:

> More generally, I will continue to rejoice at the Holy Father's decision, since this cannot fail to have consequences even outside the liturgy, in the name of the adage that links the *lex orandi* with the *lex credendi*. The prejudice in favor of a rupture that has affected the liturgy in such a grotesque way has damaged much more profoundly the relation of Catholics to their spiritual and doctrinal heritage. Where the masters who were behind the beginning of the theological renewal of the mid-twentieth century (Romano Guardini, Henri de Lubac, Hans Urs von Balthasar, Gaston Fessard, Jean Daniélou, Louis Bouyer, and so many others) were trying to broaden the contact with the tradition of the Church, their clumsy imitators have claimed to indict the most constant expressions of the Church's faith, judged henceforth unacceptable by *men of today*.[3]

---

the pastoral attitude of the Church is not dependent on arithmetical criteria: Does not the Church struggle to assert some particular liturgical expression in an Oriental rite in some particular country where Catholics are marginalized and, even so, number no more than . . . four thousand faithful?

[3] "Pourquoi je me réjouis de l'indulte", *France Catholique*, July 6, 2007.

This act of the Magisterium does in fact come in a direct line from the fundamental speech that Benedict XVI made to the Roman Curia on December 22, 2005, on the fortieth anniversary of the closing of the Second Vatican Council.

The Holy Father suggested then that we should distinguish between a *hermeneutic of discontinuity and rupture* and a *hermeneutic of reform*:

> It all depends on the correct interpretation of the Council, or—as we would say today—on its proper hermeneutics, the correct key to its interpretation and application. The problems in its implementation arose from the fact that two contrary hermeneutics came face to face and quarrelled with each other. One caused confusion, the other, silently but more and more visibly, bore and is bearing fruit. On the one hand, there is an interpretation that I would call "a hermeneutic of discontinuity and rupture"; it has frequently availed itself of the sympathies of the mass media and also one trend of modern theology. On the other, there is the "hermeneutic of reform", of renewal in the continuity of the one subject-Church which the Lord has given to us. She is a subject which increases in time and develops, yet always remaining the same, the one subject of the journeying People of God. The hermeneutic of discontinuity risks ending in a split between the pre-conciliar Church and the post-conciliar Church.

We should take another look at the lengthy exposition he devotes to this question, for this is perhaps actually the key to interpreting Benedict XVI's pontificate. This speech, which might be called practically a *keynote speech*, invites us to distance ourselves so as to grasp what is really at stake with this motu proprio: above and beyond a *concession* being made to those of the faithful attached to the old form of the Roman Missal, there are instructions about every way of celebrating the liturgy, starting with its ordinary form, according to a logic of continuity and not of rupture. And these are far from being some minor details precisely on account of the status of the liturgy as "source and summit of the life and mission of the Church", according to the well-known formula from the Second Vatican Council, which was the subject of discussion at the last ordinary synod of bishops on the Eucharist.

In his post-synodal apostolic exhortation *Sacramentum Caritatis*, Benedict XVI evaluates the reception of the liturgical reform and specifies, "Concretely, the changes which the Council called for need to be understood within the overall unity of the historical development of the rite itself, without the introduction of artificial discontinuities" (§ 3).[4] The Council's reflections on this are in fact situated within the context of the living tradition. Tradition, as Benedict XVI loves to say, is not a box of dead things, but a river springing from the very mystery of Christ, which, through the doctrine, worship, and life of the Church, continues to irrigate all the succeeding generations here on earth.[5]

Without going so far as to advocate a *reform of the reform* such as Joseph Cardinal Ratzinger used to wish for, there is no doubt that this motu proprio will be one way of resuming the work of updating and further study that the liturgical reform of the Second Vatican Council undertook. The many works on the liturgy published by Joseph Cardinal Ratzinger in recent years bear eloquent witness to the fact that this is the Holy Father's intention. Deliberately taking up the title of a famous book by Romano Guardini, which he considers to have been the starting point for the liturgical

[4] And in a footnote he explicitly refers to his speech of December 22, 2005, to the Roman Curia.

[5] Cf. the general audiences of May 3 and May 10, 2006.

movement in Germany, he closes the preface of *The Spirit of the Liturgy* with these words: "If this book were to encourage, in a new way, something like a 'liturgical movement', a movement toward the liturgy and toward the right way of celebrating the liturgy, inwardly and outwardly, then the intention that inspired its writing would be richly fulfilled."[6]

2. Which Liturgical Reform?

a. Some key elements in the liturgical movement

The Second Vatican Council's Constitution *Sacrosanctum Concilium* cannot be dissociated from the liturgical movement (1909–1963) that preceded it, the main fruits of which it welcomed and canonized.[7] A few assertions drawn from the *Catechism of the Catholic Church*, or from its *Compendium*, will be sufficient for us to gather its main features.

"The liturgy is the celebration of the mystery of Christ and in particular his Paschal Mystery. Through the exercise of the priestly ministry of Jesus Christ the liturgy manifests in signs and brings about the sanctification of humankind. The public worship which is due to God is offered by the Mystical Body of Christ, that is, by its head and by its members."[8]

---

[6] Joseph Cardinal Ratzinger, *The Spirit of the Liturgy* (San Francisco: Ignatius Press, 2000), pp. 8–9. One should also look at two earlier books by the same author: *The Feast of Faith* (San Francisco: Ignatius Press, 1986) and *A New Song for the Lord: Faith in Christ and Liturgy Today* (New York: Crossroad, 1997).

[7] Cf. José Luis Gutierrez, *Liturgie* (Éditions du Laurier, 2007), chap. 1: "La Théologie de la liturgie au XXième siècle", pp. 9–23.

[8] *Compendium: Catechism of the Catholic Church* (Vatican City: Libreria Editrice Vaticana; Washington, D.C.: United States Conference of Catholic Bishops, 2006), §218.

"The liturgy as the sacred action par excellence is the summit toward which the activity of the Church is directed and it is likewise the font from which all her power flows. Through the liturgy Christ continues the work of our redemption in, with and through his Church."[9]

"It is the mystery of Christ that the Church proclaims and celebrates in her liturgy so that the faithful may live from it and bear witness to it in the world."[10]

There is no doubt that the first positive gain from the liturgical movement is the connection between the liturgy and the lives of the faithful as the source of an authentically Christian life. This is what Pius X was aiming at, in his motu proprio *Tra le Sollecitudini* (November 22, 1903), where he recommended a more active participation of the faithful—and hence one more fruitful for their Christian life—in the mysteries of worship. At the dawn of the twentieth century, there was in fact a tendency to reduce liturgy to the rites and ceremonies that surround the celebration of the sacraments. The liturgy was seen, in a manner more phenomenological than theological, from the aspect of the exterior actions of worship, as being the envelope of the sacraments, which were quite rightly seen as linked to the sanctification of the faithful—without one always being able to grasp the constitutive unity between the rite and the sacrament. Thus the faithful drew more from popular forms of piety than from the liturgy, the source of their spiritual life, to the point that liturgy and piety or devotions finally became quite separate.[11] The goal of the liturgical movement was to find a

[9] Ibid., §219.

[10] *Catechism of the Catholic Church*, 2nd ed. (Vatican City: Libreria Editrice Vaticana; Washington, D.C.: United States Conference of Catholic Bishops, 1997), §1068.

[11] It was not unusual for Missals adapted for the use of the people to provide private prayers for them to read during the course of the liturgical celebration.

way into the heart of the liturgy in order to rediscover its living core and to ensure that it was carried out on the basis of its essential being.

To do that, it was thus necessary to link the liturgy again to the mystery of salvation, whose grace the sacraments have precisely the effect of communicating to us. The first achievement of the liturgical movement was to give the liturgy a theological definition as *the worship of the Church*, in which the subject-Church is seen as an extension in history of the person and the work of Christ, the incarnate Word. It would then be shown that the liturgy is above all the celebration of the mystery of Christ and, more precisely, of his Paschal Mystery, in which is recapitulated the whole mystery of the Incarnation, which thereby acquires an essentially cultic significance: the glorification of God and the sanctification of men constitute the twofold purpose of Christ's Paschal Mystery and thus also that of the liturgy, which is at every moment the presence and communication of that mystery.

Thus, on one hand, the liturgy is the work of the whole Christ, the head and the members always united together, who offers God the perfect act of worship due to him: this is its ascending dimension. On the other hand, Christ continues, in and through the Church to exercise his priestly office in the liturgy and thus to sanctify men: this is the descending dimension of the liturgy, which was thus recovered.

Hence that fundamental assertion that opens the constitution *Sacrosanctum Concilium*, according to which "the work of our redemption is accomplished." The mystery being celebrated here is not merely a truth that is being articulated or a past event being recalled; rather, it is a salvation event that becomes present for us in the immediacy of our current existence. This is what makes the liturgy the summit and source of all Christian life, the *sacred action* that no other action in the Church can possibly equal.

We can see here the decisive contribution of someone like Lambert Beauduin (1873–1960), with the christological-ecclesiological perspective that he opened up right at the beginning of the liturgical movement[12] and that would be given official confirmation in Pius XII's encyclical *Mediator Dei.* Furthermore, the whole liturgical doctrine developed there by the Sovereign Pontiff turns upon the actualization, in the liturgy, of the exercise of Christ's unique priesthood, shared both by the ministerial priesthood of priests and by the common priesthood of the faithful.

We may also perceive the contribution of someone like Odo Casel (1886–1948), with his doctrine about mysteries: the mysteries (events) of our salvation in Christ are constantly present and active in the mysteries (rites) of the Church's liturgy.

This is also, at a deeper level, the doctrine of Pius XII's encyclical *Mystici Corporis,* which offers a foundation for this christological-ecclesiological concept of the liturgy. In the ecclesiology of communion of the Constitution *Lumen Gentium* this was developed more profoundly, in a manner not without its effect on the restoration of the Roman liturgy ordered by the Second Vatican Council, as a fulfillment of the whole liturgical movement.

---

[12] It is usual to date the beginning of the liturgical movement from the Congress held at Malines in 1909 on the initiative of Lambert Beauduin. Yet its roots reach back to the restoration of monastic life under Prosper Guéranger (1805–1875) and to the desire for reform expressed in the pontificate of Pius X (1903–1914). There is no doubt that the restoration of the Roman liturgy at Solesmes, in Latin and with Gregorian chant, was a happy change from the neo-romantic and sentimental reaction of the nineteenth century, which had of course seen itself—with some justification—as a remedy for the cold, cerebral liturgy of the Enlightenment period.

b. Sacramentum Caritatis *and the primacy of the liturgy*

The very structure of the post-synodal apostolic exhortation *Sacramentum Caritatis* shows how Benedict XVI intends to receive the heritage of the Second Vatican Council, in particular by giving the liturgy a central place in Christian life and even by "stressing the primacy of the liturgical action" (§ 34). And indeed, if the liturgy is the celebration of the Paschal Mystery of Christ, in which God is glorified and man is sanctified, what could be more important in the life of the Church? And where could the faithful better be able to find the source of their life and their mission?

Repeating on his own account the structure of the *Catechism of the Catholic Church* (minus the fourth part, on Christian prayer), Benedict XVI divides his exhortation into three parts: the Eucharist—a mystery to be believed (I); —a mystery to be celebrated (II);—a mystery to be lived (III).

An attentive reading of the exhortation shows that liturgical action is the principle of unity for the document as a whole, insofar as it is the ritual expression of the faith of the Church—the Eucharist as a mystery to be believed, *Mysterium fidei*—and at the same time the source of the Christian life, in all its implications, whether moral, social, caritative, or missionary—the Eucharist as a mystery to be lived: life and faith are intertwined in the liturgy. It is thus that the Holy Father sums up the purpose of the exhortation: "I wish here to . . . [encourage] the Christian people to deepen their understanding of the relationship between the *eucharistic mystery*, the *liturgical action*, and the *new spiritual worship* which derives from the Eucharist as the *sacrament of charity*" (§ 5).

The liturgy is not only the expression of the mystery of the faith but also its immediacy and communication in the present day of our existence;[13] beyond this, it is determinative for the whole of our Christian life by imparting to it a dimension of worship and a eucharistic form. As Monsignor Jean-François Guérin used to say in a lapidary formula that has become one of the maxims of the Community of Saint Martin, "All the Mystery of God in the Mystery of Christ; and all the Mystery of Christ in the Mystery of the Eucharist." God-Love, made manifest in the bloody sacrifice of the Cross, which is Jesus' supreme witness to love, meets us in the present day of our lives through the non-bloody envelope of the Eucharist. The Eucharist, in its turn, gives a *eucharistic form* to the whole of our life: "He laid down his life for us; and we ought to lay down our lives for the brethren" (1 Jn 3:16).[14]

The fact is that in the postconciliar Church we have witnessed a kind of dialectic opposition between the defenders of liturgical worship and the promoters of openness to the world. Because the latter went so far as to reduce the Christian life to a mere social commitment, measured by a secular interpretation of the faith, the former reacted by taking refuge in a liturgy that was rigid to the point of "rubricism", with a danger of encouraging the faithful to protect themselves from the world to an exaggerated degree. Benedict XVI puts an end to that dispute and escapes that opposition by going above it. The liturgical action should bring faith

---

[13] "The liturgical action can never be considered generically, prescinding from the mystery of faith. Our faith and the eucharistic liturgy both have their source in the same event: Christ's gift of himself in the Paschal Mystery" (*Sacramentum Caritatis*, § 34).

[14] "The liturgy is a radiant expression of the Paschal Mystery, in which Christ draws us to himself and calls us to communion. . . . The concrete way in which the truth of God's love in Christ encounters us, attracts us, and delights us, enabling us to emerge from ourselves and drawing us towards our true vocation, which is love" (ibid., § 35).

and life together. Because it is the celebration of the Paschal Mystery of Christ, who is made truly present in the midst of his people, the liturgy imparts a eucharistic shape to the whole of the Christian existence in order to make it a "spiritual worship acceptable to God". The Christian's involvement in the mission of the Church and in society does in fact take its origin in the liturgy and draws its motivation from there, to the point of being drawn into the dynamic of the loving sacrifice of Christ that is made present in it.

At the beginning of the liturgical movement there was Pope Saint Pius X's desire to restore the liturgy and make its treasures more accessible, that it might become once more the wellspring of an authentically Christian life; and this was precisely in order to meet the challenge of an increasing secularism and to encourage the faithful to consecrate the world to God. Contrary to all expectation, the implementation of the liturgical reform led to a systematic desacralization, with the liturgy letting itself be progressively overrun by the secular culture of the surrounding world and thus losing its own proper substance.

c. *The pastoral implications of the liturgical reform*

The Church's teaching may give rise to emphases that are due to the historical circumstances in which it is applied. According to the formula *lex orandi, lex credendi*, the Church's liturgical rite will always be a reflection of her faith. One cannot deny that the Second Vatican Council, enjoying the fruits of the whole movement of biblical, patristic, theological, and liturgical renewal that preceded it and prepared the way for it, brought real developments in the area of ecclesiology. The constitution *Lumen Gentium*, in line with Pope Pius XII's encyclical *Mystici Corporis*, set out the framework of an ecclesiology of communion.[15] As an immediate consequence, that also led to a better understanding of the complementarity between the different members of the Church by restoring full theological force to the distinction between the ministerial priesthood of the priests and the common priesthood of the faithful. This was not a matter, for all that, of renouncing the specific character of the ministerial priesthood, particularly in the celebration of the liturgy of the Eucharist, or the sacrificial dimension of the Mass.

What is obvious is that more emphasis was placed on its *social* dimension, in the sense that the Eucharist is the supreme expression of the Church as communion, and that there is an intrinsic link between the eucharistic Body of Christ and his Mystical Body, in which the members do not all have the same function but do all contribute to its unity. And it is the whole body, head and members, that is the subject of the liturgy: Christ and the Church—the Church of yesterday and of today[16]—and within the Church, the priests and the lay faithful. That could not fail to influence in various ways the liturgical restoration recommended by the constitution *Sacrosanctum Concilium*, by making the "fully conscious and active participation" of the lay faithful the operative principle of the reform.[17]

In order that this participation of the laity might best be realized, a certain number of measures were recommended:

[15] "The Church is in Christ like a sacrament or as a sign and instrument both of a very closely knit union with God and of the unity of the whole human race" (*Lumen Gentium*, § 1).

[16] "The liturgy is the life of prayer and worship of a single community: the mystical Body of Christ, developing through history from a certain unique source, the teaching and the saving action of Our Lord, ever active in us through Holy Spirit" (Louis Bouyer, *Liturgy and Architecture* [Notre Dame, Ind.: Univ. of Notre Dame Press, 1967], p. 3).

[17] Cf. *Sacrosanctum Concilium*, § 14. See chap. 3.

that particular provision be made for liturgical formation of
the clergy; that a certain flexibility be provided in the use of
liturgical language; that the treasures of Holy Scripture be
made more extensively available to the faithful; and that the
rite be restored by making it more sober and transparent by
the reduction of certain repetitions and gestures added to it
over the centuries.

It was nonetheless recalled that regulation of the liturgy
was exclusively the province of the Apostolic See, and, as
the laws may determine, of the bishop. Besides, there was
no question of altering in any way what was immutable and
of divine institution. Finally, restoring did not mean *revo-
lutionizing*: "There must be no innovations unless . . . care
. . . be taken that any new forms adopted should in some
way grow organically from forms already existing."[18]

d. *The* social *emphasis in the liturgy*

There is no doubt that together with an ecclesiology of
communion, the *social* quality—in the theological sense of
the term—defines the very *ethos* of the Missal produced by
the liturgical reform. It expresses in the liturgy that *ethos of
fraternity* which Joseph Ratzinger once brought forward as
specific to Christians.[19]

Essentially, his analysis led him to demonstrate that the
word *ekklesia*, in its original sense, refers not merely to the
Church, which in any case becomes a reality in the first place
in the *local community*, in which people do in fact have the
experience of fraternity, but also in the *worshipping congregation*: "The one Church", he writes, "always exists con-

[18] *Sacrosanctum Concilium*, §23.

[19] Joseph Ratzinger, *The Meaning of Christian Brotherhood*, 2nd ed. (San Francisco: Ignatius Press, 1993).

cretely in the concrete local community. The local community realizes itself as the Church in the religious assembly that is, above all in the celebration of the Eucharist."[20] In fact the Eucharist must be understood as *concorporatio cum Christi*, as the union of Christians in the one single Body of the Lord. It is in the Eucharist, thus understood as the *sacrament of fraternity*, that the feeling of brotherhood finds its source.

Joseph Ratzinger thus began to wish that the communitarian character inherent in the liturgy of the Eucharist might be made manifest even in its outward form:

> The recognition that *ekklesia* (Church) and *adelphotes* (brotherhood) are the same thing, that the Church that fulfills herself in the celebration of the Eucharist is essentially a community of brothers, compels us to celebrate the Eucharist as a rite of brotherhood in responsory dialogue—and not to have a lonely hierarchy facing a group of laymen each one of whom is shut off in his own missal or other devotional book. The Eucharist must again become visibly the sacrament of brotherhood in order to be able to achieve its full, community-creating power.

For all that, he hastened to add, "This does not imply a social dogmatism."[21]

So as to demonstrate this communitarian emphasis, the new Missal increased the number of dialogues between the priest and the faithful and provided for a more active participation by everyone in the liturgical action. It also restored the ancient kiss of peace, which expresses this wish for brotherhood, even for reconciliation, at the moment when people are going to draw the power of fraternal communion from

[20] Ibid., p. 68.
[21] Ibid., pp. 68–69.

the Sacrifice of Christ in sacramental Communion.[22] It once more made room for common prayer, known as "universal prayer", which had fallen into disuse and a vestige of which remained, in the earlier Missal in the "Oremus" preceding the offertory. Finally, it extended the opportunity for concelebration.

Permission was even given *ad experimentum*—and hence under the control of the Holy See—for adjustments in the manner of celebrating following the new Missal with respect to the social aspect of the liturgy. I am thinking in particular of the positioning of the congregation, having the sign of peace before the offertory, and the way of having communion that characterize the celebration of the Eucharist within the framework of the Neocatechumenal Way.[23]

3. The Way out of the Crisis

In paying homage to Monsignor Klaus Gamber, who up to his sudden death in 1989 was director of the Ratisbon

---

[22] On this subject, one must read the exposition devoted to the *kiss of peace* by Benedict XVI in his exhortation *Sacramentum Caritatis*, §49. We can find there, in n. 150, this most interesting suggestion for avoiding too great a diversion of the attention of the faithful at the most important moment of Communion: "Taking into account ancient and venerable customs and the wishes expressed by the Synod Fathers, I have asked the competent curial offices to study the possibility of moving the sign of peace to another place, such as before the presentation of the gifts at the altar. To do so would also serve as a significant reminder of the Lord's insistence that we be reconciled with others before offering our gifts to God (cf. *Mt* 5:23ff.)."

[23] I do not know what the position is concerning the definitive approval of this experiment by the Holy See, but it does seem that the Holy Father is referring to this type of liturgical practice in *Sacramentum Caritatis* when he mentions the "formative value" and the "catechetical value" of eucharistic celebrations in small groups, though nonetheless on condition that they are "consonant with the overall pastoral activity of the Diocese" and that they "serve to unify the community, not to fragment it" (§63).

Liturgical Institute, Joseph Cardinal Ratzinger sketched in broad outline and uncompromisingly the crisis in the liturgy we have been experiencing since the years just after the Council. Having noted that the Western liturgy is essentially *the fruit of a development*—in contrast to the Oriental liturgy, which became fixed in the fourteenth century and which seems like *the reflection of the eternal liturgy*—he noted that following the Council, "in the place of liturgy as the fruit of a continuous development came fabricated liturgy. We abandoned the living process of growth and evolution and went in for manufacturing. People no longer wanted to continue the organic process of evolution and maturation of a living thing down the centuries and replaced it— as in technological production—with a fabrication, the banal product of the moment."[24] He did not even hesitate to link the crisis in the Church with the crisis of the liturgy: "I am convinced that the crisis we are going through in the Church today is largely based on the disintegration of the liturgy, which is even sometimes conceived in such a way —*etsi Deus non daretur*—that its intention is no longer at all

---

[24] In Klaus Gamber, *Le Réforme liturgique en question* (éd. Sainte-Madeleine, 1992), pp. 6–8. In this text, entitled "Klaus Gamber, l'intrépidité d'un vrai témoin", which the editor has used as a preface to this collection of articles by the great German liturgical historian, we find these further severe remarks by Cardinal Ratzinger: "The way in which the liturgical reform was actually applied took it farther and farther away from its origins. The result was not a revival but a devastation. On one hand, there was a kind of liturgy that had degenerated into a show, in which people tried to make liturgy interesting with the help of whatever foolish business was fashionable and with enticing moral maxims; with temporary successes among the group of liturgical manufacturers and, among those who are not looking for a spiritual *showmaster* in the liturgy, but an encounter with the living God in the face of whom all *doing* becomes insignificant, an attitude of recoil all the more pronounced, because only that encounter makes it possible for us to gain access to the true wealth of being. On the other hand, there was the conservation of ritual forms whose sublimity still moves us; yet this, pushed to extremes, demonstrates an opinionated isolation and ultimately leaves us only sadness" (p. 6).

to make it known that God exists, that he speaks to us and that he listens to us."[25]

The crisis in the liturgy is essentially the loss of the sense of mystery or the sense of the sacred. *Rediscovering the sense of mystery*—that was the insistent exhortation of John Paul II in the last great documents of his pontificate to which we have already referred;[26] it is also the fundamental recommendation of Benedict XVI in his motu proprio. So how do we get out of the crisis? That is the question we should like to try to answer here: the essence will consist of exploring the path opened up by the motu proprio.

a. A mutual enrichment of the two Missals

In his encyclical *Ecclesia de Eucharistia*, John Paul II made this statement: "At times one encounters an extremely reductive understanding of the Eucharistic mystery. Stripped of its sacrificial meaning, it is celebrated as if it were simply a fraternal banquet. Furthermore, the necessity of the ministerial priesthood, grounded in apostolic succession, is at times obscured and the sacramental nature of the Eucharist is reduced to its mere effectiveness as a form of proclamation. . . . The Eucharist is too great a gift to tolerate ambiguity and depreciation" (§ 10).[27] Indeed, the great emphasis

[25] Joseph Ratzinger, *Milestones: Memoirs 1927–1977* (San Francisco: Ignatius Press, 1998).

[26] See the encyclical letter *Ecclesia de Eucharistia*, 2003, in particular chap. 5 on the dignity of the eucharistic celebration; and the apostolic exhortation *Ecclesia in Europa*, 2003, §§ 67–73.

[27] He insistently repeats this in his encyclical: "The 'treasure' is too important and precious to risk impoverishment or compromise through forms of experimentation or practices introduced without a careful review on the part of the competent ecclesiastical authorities" (§ 51). "No one is permitted to undervalue the mystery entrusted to our hands: it is too great for anyone

on the *social* character of the Eucharist, said to be one of the major achievements of the liturgical movement, often went hand-in-hand, in practice, with a loss of the sacrificial sense of the Mass and with a minimizing of the role of the priest in the eucharistic celebration.

Here we come to a significant demonstration of the *hermeneutic of discontinuity* denounced by Benedict XVI. Now, further theological study of Vatican II must be situated within a logic of growth and not of rupture:[28] the increased emphasis on the communal character of the liturgy, which was the product of the ecclesiology of communion expounded by the Council, was not offered as an alternative to the intrinsically sacrificial dimension of the Mass or to the importance of the ministerial priesthood, particularly stressed by the Missal promulgated following the Council of Trent.[29] The fact is that the dogmatic contribution of this latter Council concerning transubstantiation, the holy sacrifice of the Mass, and the ministerial priesthood of the priest was not solely motivated circumstantially by the errors being spread abroad at the time of the Reformation, but constituted in a more positive way the *unwrapping* of truths that had for a long time remained implicit in the revealed message and were nonetheless held as true by the faithful

---

to feel free to treat it lightly and with disregard for its sacredness and its universality" (§ 52).

[28] In the letter to the bishops he wrote to accompany his motu proprio *Summorum Pontificum*, Benedict XVI writes, "In the history of the liturgy there is growth and progress, but no rupture."

[29] "Though the idea of a 'banquet' naturally suggests familiarity, the Church has never yielded to the temptation to trivialize this 'intimacy' with her Spouse by forgetting that he is also her Lord and that the 'banquet' always remains a sacrificial banquet marked by the blood shed on Golgotha. *The Eucharistic Banquet is truly a 'sacred' banquet*, in which the simplicity of the signs conceals the unfathomable holiness of God" (*Ecclesia de Eucharistia*, § 48).

people. The Protestant Reformation was merely the *historical condition* for these dogmatic definitions, and not their *proper cause*, which must be sought at a deeper level in the *charism of aid* enjoyed by the supreme Magisterium of the Church, which urges it to grasp the content of the faith at an ever deeper level. Thus these doctrines are still of current relevance.

In that sense, the motu proprio *Summorum Pontificum* is counting on the mutual enrichment of the two forms of the Roman Missal. If the Missal known as that of Saint Pius V has a more sacrificial and hierarchical *temperament*—bearing in mind the ecclesial context we have just recalled—conserving it as an extraordinary form could well have the beneficial effect that "celebration of the Mass according to the Missal of Paul VI will be able to demonstrate, more powerfully than has been the case hitherto, the sacrality which attracts many people to the former usage."[30]

A few months before the publication of this motu proprio, Father François Cassingena-Trévedy, making a remarkable "Outline of a Comparative Genealogy", suggested much the same.[31] He showed in convincing fashion that, if the Tridentine liturgy is related on the whole to an Antiochene and Dionysian tradition that lends it an essentially "transcendent and hierarchical" tone, one "of mysteries", the liturgy as restored under Paul VI moved more toward the pole of a "social, ministerial" ecclesiology, "that of community", of an Augustinian type. The interesting thing about his analysis

[30] Letter of His Holiness Benedict XVI to the bishops, to accompany the motu proprio; cf. appendix.

[31] François Cassingena-Trévedy, *Te Igitur* (Geneva: Ad Solem, 2007), chap. 6, pp. 73–82. Father Cassingena-Trévedy is a Benedictine monk at Ligugé; he teaches liturgy at the Institut Supérieur de liturgie of the Paris Institut Catholique.

is that he relates both of these concepts of liturgy, as they appear in the two Missals, to tradition: "Certainly, these are differing concepts, but not contradictory. For it is important to emphasize yet again, above all else, that the two genealogical lines we have tried to identify in the two Missals are equally traditional, the one just as much as the other, and that consequently they are entitled to the same consideration and to the same affection."[32] According to him, the difference between the two Missals is less a matter of their contents, of the actual texts, than of their respective temperaments: this is a matter of two "ethoses of celebration . . . one belonging to the sphere of *absolute liturgy*, and the other to that of liturgy *related to the world*".[33] We have in fact remarked to what extent the restoration of the Roman Missal ordered by the Second Vatican Council was linked to the prevailing intention of the liturgical movement to make the liturgy the source of an authentically Christian life—especially in order to meet the challenge of the growing secularism that has characterized the world since the beginning of the twentieth century.

In an almost prophetic manner, the writer concluded,

That being so, it would be highly desirable . . . for the ethoses of celebration, the *social* type and that of *mystery* (in the most solidly theological sense one can give to these two terms) finally to become acquainted with each other in order to be mutually enriched with their own specific character. In short, it is highly desirable that instead of remaining isolated in our respective attachments, we analyze their origins in the light of tradition, that our attachments should visit with each other.[34]

[32] Ibid., pp. 81–82.
[33] Ibid., p. 81.
[34] Ibid., p. 82.

In his motu proprio, Benedict XVI seems to appropriate this interesting suggestion. To do this, it is certainly necessary for the two Missals to be called to live together.

b. A greater fidelity to liturgical norms

We will not escape the crisis unless we return to a greater fidelity to liturgical norms. To that end, an attentive rereading of the major documents of the conciliar reform is indispensable, starting with the constitution *Sacrosanctum Concilium*, which defines the general principles that must govern the restoration of the Roman liturgy. Besides that, a study of the *General Instruction of the Roman Missal* is highly desirable.[35] Here, the apostolic exhortation *Sacramentum Caritatis*, issued just a few months earlier than the motu proprio, offers us some invaluable suggestions.

THE ART OF CELEBRATING WELL

In a society closed to transcendence, the mission awaiting the Church in Europe, said John Paul II, "consists in rediscovering the sense of 'mystery'; in renewing liturgical celebrations to that they can be more eloquent signs of the presence of Christ the Lord".[36] He added, "The purpose of the liturgy of the Church is not to placate people's desires or fears, but to hear and receive the living Jesus, who honors and praises the Father, in order that we may praise

---

[35] Recommending that people read this, Benedict XVI writes, "Perhaps we take it for granted that our ecclesial communities already know and appreciate these resources [the great riches found in the *General Instruction of the Roman Missal* and the *Order of Readings for Mass*], but this is not always the case" (*Sacramentum Caritatis*, § 40).

[36] *Ecclesia in Europa*, § 69.

and honor the Father with him." He invites us "once more to put Jesus at the center" of liturgical celebrations.[37]

It is the mystery of Christ that is the living heart of liturgical celebration: only the Church, his Bride, is commensurate with the mystery of her Bridegroom, and consequently she alone can determine, from within the mystery in which she participates supernaturally, the rules for the liturgy. Besides that, the Church, the unique subject-Church, grows through time in organic fashion, without rupture. We can understand, then, why observance of the liturgical norms laid down by the Church is so important, in order for our celebrations to be ever "more eloquent signs of the presence of Christ the Lord".

In his exhortation, *Sacramentum Caritatis*, Benedict XVI puts great emphasis on the *ars celebrandi*, the art of celebrating well, which "is the fruit of faithful adherence to the liturgical norms in all their richness" and is "the primary way to foster the participation of the People of God in the sacred rite".[38] These reflections on the *ars celebrandi* are preceded by a fine exposition of the connection between *beauty* and *liturgy*: beauty is "not mere decoration, but rather an essential element of the liturgical action".[39] Thus, the source of the art of celebrating well is intrinsic to the liturgy itself: the beauty of which the rite wishes only to be the manifestation is that of Christ himself in his Paschal Mystery.[40] All artistic expression thus finds its principal source of inspiration in

---

[37] Ibid., §71.

[38] *Sacramentum Caritatis*, §38.

[39] Ibid., §35.

[40] "The 'subject' of the liturgy's intrinsic beauty is Christ himself, risen and glorified in the Holy Spirit, who includes the Church in his work" (ibid., §36).

faith in the Christ who died and rose again, and this is the supreme criterion for authentic sacred art.[41] The liturgical norms, far from imposing constraints of an exterior and legalistic kind, thus become guarantors of this intrinsic beauty of the liturgy and "express . . . , on the part of the minister, a docile openness to receiving this ineffable gift".[42]

Thus it is emphasized that the liturgy is first of all an object for wonder and contemplation—and not for fabrication, as if it were material at the disposal of our own hands. In that sense, there is no doubt that the rediscovery of eucharistic adoration is a more than positive development, hailed as much by John Paul II as by Benedict XVI. The practice of adoration can in fact become a fine way of rediscovering the sense of mystery in the eucharistic celebration: "Eucharistic adoration is simply the natural consequence of the eucharistic celebration, which is itself the Church's supreme act of adoration."[43]

The role of the bishop as *moderator of the liturgy* within his diocese is greatly emphasized—that is to say, his jurisdiction, with his capacity to authorize things or to forbid them or even to take disciplinary actions. But has the exemplary character of this task in this area been sufficiently emphasized? Benedict XVI recalls that he ought to be the "celebrant par excellence within his Diocese" and urges that "every effort be made to ensure that the liturgies which the Bishop celebrates in his Cathedral are carried out with complete respect for the *ars celebrandi*, so that they can be considered an example for the entire Diocese."[44]

---

[41] Cf. ibid., §§41–42, on art "placed at the service of the celebration" and "liturgical song". See also *Ecclesia de Eucharistia*, §§49–51.

[42] *Sacramentum Caritatis*, §40.

[43] Ibid., §66.

[44] Ibid., §39. The members of the liturgical commission of the diocese, like

REDISCOVERING THE SACRED
GESTURES OF THE ROMAN RITE

"Equally important for a correct *ars celebrandi* is an attentive-ness to the various kinds of language that the liturgy em-ploys: words and music, gestures and silence, movement, the liturgical colors of the vestments." And Benedict XVI adds, "The simplicity of its gestures and the sobriety of its orderly sequence of signs communicate and inspire more than any contrived and inappropriate additions."[45]

It is here in particular, in the sacred gestures, that we most strongly have the impression of a break with tradition in im-plementing the liturgical reform. Whereas the gestures that came to us from the depths of the distant past, especially from the golden age of the Roman liturgy, had the means to immerse us in one moment in the mystery by taking us out of the profane world that always tends to turn us away from God, in their place people have put instead, often from a lack of formation, artificial and stereotyped gestures, bor-rowed from ordinary life and incapable of opening to the transcendence of the mystery being celebrated.[46]

One of the ways to get out of the crisis would be to rediscover the beauty of the sacred gestures linked to the old form of the Roman rite, which have not been abolished

---

those of the commissions of sacred art and of sacred music, should be chosen with care; they should be provided with the means to keep a real watch over the parishes and to be available to them for advice, no less than for making the bishop's liturgy a good example: cf. *Sacrosanctum Concilium*, §§45–46.

[45] *Sacramentum Caritatis*, §40.

[46] And whenever people object that certain signs or gestures were associ-ated with a given era, sometimes for utilitarian purposes, I reply in the words of Cardinal Newman: "When a sign is associated with some particular era, it should be abandoned unless it has subsequently been enriched with new significance."

on the pretext of their having been simplified in the new Missal. Here I am in agreement with François Cassingena-Trévedy's analysis in his study of the Missal of Saint Pius V. On condition that it be carried out lovingly and with interior recollection, "with full mystagogic awareness and in hereditary solidarity with other venerable liturgical families . . . this ritual *activity* . . . no longer amounts to a nervous twitch in the liturgy but is, quite on the contrary, a grace."[47] And the writer bases what he says on a fundamental anthropological consideration: "The attachment currently felt for the Tridentine rite raises questions about a certain neglect, for the past thirty years, of the legitimate anthropological component—and thus the element of gesture—in the liturgy: a neglect that seems paradoxical when one is aware of the general respect for the human sciences, a neglect that is especially a matter of prejudice."[48] And we may indeed deplore "the inconsistency of gesture that often characterizes our contemporary manner of celebrating". He then concludes, "For however strange it may seem, in a culture that uses and abuses the body, we no longer know what to do with the body liturgically, so that our ethos of celebration is a curious mixture of ideological disincarnation and individualistic invention of gestures that have no true point of reference."[49]

Experience in fact shows that, far from imposing constraints on the celebrant, on the contrary, the precision of these ritual gestures sets him free to become fully involved in the mystery he is celebrating and offers the faithful a greater interior freedom to bring themselves into the presence of Christ the Lord. The noble and solemn weight of

[47] *Te Igitur*, p. 69.
[48] Ibid., p. 70.
[49] Ibid.

the hieratic ritual of the old Missal brought the celebrant to efface himself before the One whom it was his mission to make manifest to the world. Whereas the absence of a codified ritual condemns the celebrant to a creativity that is in danger of drawing attention to his own personality rather than to Christ, of whom he is called by his vocation to be the servant and the sacrament.

FINDING ROOM ONCE MORE FOR GREGORIAN CHANT

The more or less general suppression of Gregorian chant in the Roman liturgy since the liturgical reform is surprising, as if this chant, whose history goes back more than a thousand years and which is so deeply embedded in the texture of the Roman rite, had suddenly become obsolete. When we note the musical and doctrinal poverty of the hymns that flourished in the years just following the Council, such disaffection is all the more distressing.

The fact is that sacred music has suffered the effects of a *misunderstanding* of the active participation asked for by the Council. It is true that the first liturgical movement had at first emphasized participation of the faithful through singing, and one can understand why. In order to put a stop to an inflation of musical artistry, which had sometimes become elitist, people aimed at a certain simplicity. There developed then a distinction between what people call *esoteric music* (in the positive sense of the term) and *utilitarian music*. As for simplicity, banality and superficiality have not been avoided, and on the pretext of the active participation of the assembly of the faithful, Church hymns have become quasi-profane songs, incapable of lifting hearts, hardly fit for stirring the senses and in any case incapable of serving the purpose of the liturgy—that is, the glorification of God and the sanctification and edification of the faithful.

That is not what the Council, which devoted a chapter of its constitution *Sacrosanctum Concilium* to sacred music and decreed exact rules, had called for. The most authoritative commentary on this magisterial text is the *chirograph* of John Paul II on the occasion of the centenary of Saint Pius X's motu proprio *Tra le Sollecitudini*, which was in fact on sacred music. John Paul II repeats there that Gregorian chant, "being especially suited to the Roman Liturgy" should, "other things being equal", be given pride of place in liturgical services.[50] It is still today, as it were, "the supreme model of sacred music" and "an element of unity in the Roman Liturgy".[51] Benedict XVI reaffirms this, in *Sacramentum Caritatis*: "Finally . . . I desire, in accordance with the request advanced by the Synod Fathers, that Gregorian chant be suitably esteemed and employed as the chant proper to the Roman liturgy."[52] Do we not have the right to demand that such authoritative calls be heard, that Gregorian chant be included once more in the clergy's formation program, and that it regain its favored place in the repertory of our ordinary liturgical assemblies? Especially inasmuch as the Gregorian *Kyries*, for example, are not only not an obstacle to the participation of the faithful, but, on the contrary, encourage it by creating a unanimity that is quite appropriate to the communal nature of the liturgy.

There is in fact no opposition between the beauty of sacred song, starting with Gregorian chant—not neglecting polyphonic music, for which Palestrina is still the model, or even more modern or contemporary compositions, provided they are in harmony with the meaning and the spirit of the liturgy—and participation of the faithful. The Coun-

---

[50] Cf. *Sacrosanctum Concilium*, §116.

[51] Chirograph, §7.

[52] *Sacrosanctum Concilium*, §42.

cil did in fact promote the creation of choirs or *scholae canto-rum*, in cathedral churches in particular, that could both assist the active participation of the congregation and provide the proper parts that require more professional skill. Besides, even when the *schola* is performing the proper parts, the participation of the faithful is no less requisite: listening, responding, and being moved are activities in the same way as speaking and singing. That is what led Cardinal Ratzinger to say, "In more concrete terms, there are a good number of people who can sing better 'with the heart' than 'with their mouths', but their hearts are really stimulated to sing through the singing of those who *have* the gift of singing 'with their mouths'. It is as if they themselves actually sing in the others; thankful listening is united with the voices of the singers in the one worship of God."[53]

It was Cardinal Ratzinger, again, who emphasized that it is paradoxical to insist so much nowadays on the inculturation of the liturgy in the specific spirit, including that of the music, of the regions where Christianity is taking root while at the same time so systematically choosing to overlook sacred music that is so symbolic of our Western culture.

MORE CLEARLY EMPHASIZING THE CONNECTION BETWEEN THE BIBLE AND THE LITURGY

The Second Vatican Council had expressed the wish "that the intimate connection between words and rites may be apparent in the liturgy". Thus, it is quite right to consider the enlargement of the lectionary as one of the special treasures of the new Missal.[54] Did the Council not ask that the faithful

[53] *The Feast of Faith*, trans. Graham Harrison (San Francisco: Ignatius Press, 1986), p. 124.

[54] *Sacrosanctum Concilium*, §35; cf. ibid., "In sacred celebrations there is to be more reading from holy scripture, and it is to be more varied and suitable."

might have more access to the treasures of Holy Scripture in the liturgy? The liturgy is in fact an entirely separate organ of the tradition and transmits to us the living proclamation of the apostles; in this way, it is the place above all others for the reception of the word of God, where Holy Scripture —which is the word written down under the inspiration of the Holy Spirit—becomes a living and life-giving word for today. There is no doubt that it is in this way that we can best inherit the fruits of the liturgical reform. And nothing should be given preference over Holy Scripture—not only for the readings as such, but also for the songs and canticles and even for the rituals whose underlying meaning is given precisely by Scripture. There is a great deal to be done in ridding the musical repertoire of our assemblies of those compositions that are intended to be poetic but remain insipid and hollow for want of being inspired by Scripture. Similarly, a good many liturgical gestures have been sacrificed out of a lack of thorough understanding of their origin in Scripture and in the history of salvation. In any case, that is not what was called for by the Council when it recommended that the word of God should permeate the whole of the liturgy: readings, songs, and rituals.

Doubtless the old Missal opened the treasures of the Bible less generously, but the repetition of the Sunday texts during the week did perhaps allow the faithful to assimilate the word more completely, and, above all, the songs of the Mass —introit, gradual, alleluia or processional, offertory hymn, hymn at communion—always drawn from Scripture, mainly from the Old Testament and especially from the Psalms, constituted a commentary of Scripture by Scripture. There was a whole liturgical catechism there, the impact of which should not be underestimated and which has been preserved in the *Graduale Romanum*, which Pope Pius X had restored precisely in order to facilitate a better participation of the faithful.

A MORE TRADITIONAL USE
OF THE EUCHARISTIC PRAYERS

As for the use made of the four eucharistic prayers provided initially in the new Missal, we have to admit that in practice it is the second that is most often, or even systematically, used to the detriment of the three others, and especially the first, known as the *Roman canon*, which comes straight out of the old Missal: on the pretext that the latter is a heterogeneous and later composition, unless it is to avoid its length (sic). Here we are touching on one of the most tenacious prejudices, connected with the state of liturgical studies at the time of the reform (1970), which claimed that the second eucharistic prayer was the most ancient: it was said to be found, just as we have it, in the *Apostolic Tradition* of Hippolytus. Now, advances in historical and liturgical studies show, on the contrary, that it is the Roman canon that is the most ancient, as it offers semitisms that are very consistent with the liturgical formulae developed from the practices of the first Jewish Christian communities. So the relationship with Old Testament liturgy is well shown.[55]

---

[55] Cf. Louis Bouyer, *Eucharist*, trans. Charles Underhill Quinn (Notre Dame, Ind.: Univ of Notre Dame Press, 1968), especially chap. 7, "The Alexandrian and Roman Eucharists", pp. 187–243: "Put back thus in its true context, the Roman canon appears then as one of the most venerable witnesses of the oldest tradition of the eucharistic prayer, at least contemporary in its totality with the most archaic forms of the Alexandrian eucharist. There is every reason to think that the succession of these prayers and their content with many key expressions go straight back to the assuredly very ancient time at which the eucharist at Rome as everywhere else was definitively connected with the service of readings and prayers. That is to say that Hippolytus, far from being its originator—a man who still wished to ignore this connection—must have propagated his own rite in Rome, if he ever did

As for the other eucharistic prayers, we know that even if their doctrinal value is beyond question, their composition involved extensive borrowing from Oriental and Gallican liturgical traditions, and they thus appear as alien bodies in a Roman rite whose growth up till then had always been homogenous and without any break.[56]

One might perhaps suggest a distribution of the four eucharistic prayers that would allow us to diminish the impression of a break with tradition: for example, reserving the Roman canon for Sundays, feast days and solemnities of the Lord and of the Virgin Mary and those of all the saints mentioned in the *communicantes* and the *nobis quoque*. The second might be better adapted to weekday Masses, the third to the commemorations of saints, and the fourth, with its compulsory preface, for Friday, in memory of the Passion of Jesus as the fulfillment of the whole history of salvation.

DISPELLING A MISUNDERSTANDING
ABOUT NONEXISTENT RULES

If people take great liberties with liturgical norms nowadays, there are paradoxically two *prohibitions* that seem to have been imposed in the course of implementing the reform: that of the use of Latin, and that of Mass oriented toward the east, toward God.

Concerning Latin, the constitution *Sacrosanctum Concilium* is content to remind us, on the contrary, that, ''particular

---

so, only in a vain attempt to dislodge a rite which must already have been very like the one that has come down to us and which we still use, with the exception that the language was still Greek and not Latin'' (p. 243).

[56] This was the opinion of the liturgical historian Klaus Gamber, in *The Reform of the Roman Liturgy: Its Problems and Background*, trans. Klaus D. Grimm (San Juan Capistrano, Calif.: Una Voce Press; Harrison, N.Y.: Foundation for Catholic Reform, 1993), p. 55.

law remaining in force, the use of the Latin language is to be preserved in the Latin rites",[57] and that "nevertheless steps should be taken so that the faithful may also be able to say or to sing together in Latin those parts of the Ordinary of the Mass which pertain to them."[58] Benedict XVI recalls this in his exhortation, suggesting it in particular for large international celebrations, so as to manifest more clearly the unity of the universal Church.[59] It is the vernacular language that is offered as a possibility, especially for readings, for instructions, and for prayers like the prayer of the faithful, so as to make it easy for the faithful to understand. Between that and forbidding Latin, as has been done, lies a reaction of an ideological order that is hardly acceptable. Given all that, one understands why most people identify *the Mass in Latin* with *the Mass of Saint Pius V.*

Concerning the orientation of the celebration, we find nothing in the Council's constitution, merely the possibility mentioned in the *General Instruction of the Roman Missal.*[60] Scholarly studies since then have shown, besides, that—contrary to what had been asserted at the time—the Mass *versus populum,* in the final analysis, has no historical foundation and that turning east toward the Lord is known not merely to be more in line with the best-established tradition, but also to have a wealth of very profound mystagogical significance.[61]

[57] *Sacrosanctum Concilium,* § 36:1.

[58] Ibid., § 54.

[59] Cf. *Sacramentum Caritatis,* § 62.

[60] Cf. *General Instruction of the Roman Missal,* § 299: "The altar should be built apart from the wall, in such a way that it is possible to walk around it easily and that Mass can be celebrated at it facing the people, which is desirable wherever possible."

[61] May I be permitted here simply to refer to Joseph Ratzinger, *The Spirit of the Liturgy* (San Francisco: Ignatius Press, 2000), pp. 74–84; Uwe Michael

There is no doubt it will be difficult—and not always desirable from the pastoral point of view—to change things radically, given the extent to which this prejudice is embedded in habits and thinking; yet it should at least be allowed once more to celebrate facing God, on condition that this be reintroduced pedagogically. It will in any case be necessary to give again the christological basis of orientation in prayer, including its use in celebrations *versus populum*. As Cardinal Ratzinger suggested, we ought at least to replace the cross, in a conspicuous way, between the celebrant and the faithful: "The cross on the altar is not obstructing the view; it is a common point of reference. It is an open "iconostasis" which, far from hindering unity, actually facilitates it: it is the image which draws and unites the attention of everyone. I would even be so bold as to suggest that the cross on the altar is actually a necessary precondition for celebrating toward the people."[62]

c. *Greater care given to liturgical formation*

John Paul II used to assert that the genuine renewal of the liturgy would demand a great effort in training everyone, ordained ministers, consecrated persons, and laypeople: "Aimed at fostering an understanding of the true meaning of the Church's liturgical celebrations, it requires, in addition to an adequate instruction in the rites, an authentic spirituality and formation in experiencing those celebrations fully."[63]

An emphasis on liturgical formation, beginning with that of the clergy, is one of the fruits of the liturgical movement.

Lang, *Turning towards the Lord: Orientation in Liturgical Prayer* (San Francisco: Ignatius Press, 2004); and even Louis Bouyer, *Liturgy and Architecture*.

[62] *The Feast of Faith*, p. 145.

[63] *Ecclesia in Europa*, §73.

Pope Benedict XVI, in his letter to the bishops on the occasion of the *motu proprio*, highlights the fact that an attachment to the earlier form of the Roman rite is especially to be found "where the liturgical movement had provided many people with a notable liturgical formation". And he recognizes that "the use of the old Missal presupposes a certain degree of liturgical formation" and that "neither" this nor a knowledge of Latin "is found very often" nowadays.

THE LITURGY IN SEMINARIES

Because of the dialectical oppositions that have poisoned the life of the Church in France in the years since the Council and that have become focused around the *lectern*, it seems that in seminaries cut-rate liturgy has been the choice. Aiming at a "happy medium" that often borders on mediocrity, quite simply forgetting to make the liturgy "the source and the summit" of the whole of Christian life. Under the pretext of avoiding a certain liturgical sensitivity, even a rubricism, which it is not unusual to encounter in a good many seminarians, they made the liturgy excessively austere instead of educating in the true sense of liturgy. They did try, with the best of intentions, to give the liturgy pride of place before other forms of personal piety; yet in doing this, they, sometimes systematically, disposed of *pious exercises*, whereas the Council had merely demanded that these be "imbued with the spirit of the liturgy".[64] This was done in favor of a liturgy that was so cerebral and so little mystagogical that in the best cases it became the place for the seminarians to pursue their personal piety. From the cerebralism of a liturgy influenced by the Enlightenment, they passed to the sentimentality of a liturgy inspired by Romanticism. In these conditions, what

[64] *Sacrosanctum Concilium*, § 17.

happened to the great inspiration of the liturgical movement —or, more precisely, *the spirit of the liturgy* that, beyond cold reasoning or exaggerated sensibility, goes back to the very soul of the Church?

The Council's constitution on the sacred liturgy presented liturgical formation as one of the fundamental principles for the restoration and promotion of the liturgy. "Yet it would be futile to entertain any hopes of realizing this unless the pastors themselves, in the first place, became thoroughly imbued with the spirit and power of the liturgy and undertake to give instruction about it."[65] This was no doubt a matter of training qualified professors and even of making liturgy one of the "principal courses" of ecclesiastical studies.[66] It was emphasized, nonetheless, that this formation should not be purely intellectual or theological, but that it should come by way of an authentic experience of the liturgy of the Church:

> In seminaries and houses of religious, clerics shall be given a liturgical formation in their spiritual life. For this they will need proper direction, so that they may be able to understand the sacred rites and take part in them wholeheartedly; and they will also need personally to celebrate the sacred mysteries, as well as popular devotions which are imbued with the spirit of the liturgy. In addition they must learn how to observe the liturgical laws, so that life in seminaries and houses of religious may be thoroughly influenced by the spirit of the liturgy.[67]

And indeed, before being an object of study, liturgy is a life. It is the heart par excellence of all formation in the Christian life: in the sense of faith and the sense of the Church,

[65] Ibid., §14.
[66] Ibid., §16.
[67] Ibid., §17.

in praise and adoration as in mission. Thus one could not celebrate a cut-rate liturgy: it would be the true center and summit of all seminary life, which should be structured by it.

The understanding and concrete experience of the rites, in loving conformity to the liturgical norms, attention to the degrees of solemnity of the liturgical seasons and days, even in the arrangement of sacred space, the exemplary *ars celebrandi* of the celebrants, the active participation of the seminarians in the liturgical service, with regular practice, experience of sacred chant, and the formation of a choir, the care given to objects used in worship and to vestments, all of this will contribute to making the liturgy the source and the summit of seminary life.

One does not participate in the liturgy in the same way one attends some other exercise: that must be manifest, even in bodily attitudes and in one's manner of dress.[68] It is a communal act that demands common gestures, capable of making manifest the unity of the Mystical Body of Christ: Tell me how you celebrate and how you participate in the liturgy, and I will tell you *who* your community is: a congenial collection of individuals or the Church of Christ!

Finally, Benedict XVI insists on a formation in the history of art as an important subject, "with special reference to sacred buildings and the corresponding liturgical norms".[69] Similarly, he asks "that future priests, from their time in the seminary, receive the preparation needed to understand and to celebrate Mass in Latin, and also to use Latin texts and execute Gregorian chant".[70]

---

[68] Why not arrange things so that the seminarians ordinarily wear choir robes for the liturgy, at least starting from their admission to the seminary?

[69] *Sacramentum Caritatis*, §41.

[70] Ibid., §62.

THE LITURGICAL FORMATION OF THE FAITHFUL

The Council requested, furthermore, that care be taken in the liturgical formation of the faithful, a task that falls particularly to pastors and that is indissolubly linked with the exterior and interior participation in the liturgy we wish to promote. The *active* participation of the faithful requires a *conscious* participation, and that demands a sound knowledge of the liturgical rites, closely associated with the mystery being celebrated. Similarly, this active participation is not completed within the liturgical action but extends into daily life, giving it a *cultic shape*: that is *fruitful* participation in the liturgy.

In his apostolic exhortation, Benedict XVI emphasizes the need to provide a *mystagogical catechesis* for the faithful that will always consist of three elements: "*It interprets the rites in the light of the events of our salvation*", that is to say, of the history of salvation that is recapitulated in Christ and that is really fulfilled in the liturgy through gestures, words, and silences; the need for "*presenting the meaning of the signs contained in the rites*", especially since these signs are not part of everyday life and because their vocation is to turn hearts and minds toward the transcendence of the mystery being celebrated;[71] finally, the concern "with bringing out the *significance of the rites for the Christian life*", of which the liturgy is above all else the source.[72]

---

[71] One recalls the remarkable mystagogical catechesis given by Benedict XVI on liturgical vestments in his homily at the Chrism Mass on Holy Thursday, April 5, 2007: "I would therefore like to explain to you, dear Confreres, on this Holy Thursday, the essence of the priestly ministry, interpreting the liturgical vestments themselves, which are precisely intended to illustrate what 'putting on Christ', what speaking and acting *in persona Christi*, mean."

[72] *Sacramentum Caritatis*, §64. For a good explanation of the rites, gestures,

As Benedict XVI has written, "the best catechesis on the Eucharist is the Eucharist itself, celebrated well",[73] as if meaning that the *ars celebrandi* is the first mystagogical catechesis. The celebrant will count particularly on the homily to give this catechesis; this is not so much a matter of displaying one's exegetical erudition as relying on the word proclaimed and the rites displayed to introduce the faithful to an understanding of the holy mysteries and touch their hearts so as to bring about their conversion: "Generic and abstract homilies should be avoided. In particular, I ask these ministers to preach in such a way that the homily closely relates the proclamation of the word of God to the sacramental celebration and the life of the community, so that the word of God truly becomes the Church's vital nourishment and support."[74]

Liturgical teams could be the preferred place for this mystagogical catechesis, on condition that one does not give the impression of *fabricating* the liturgy. So as to facilitate the exterior and interior participation of the assembled faithful through the functions they perform—preparation of the altar or floral decorations, proclamation of the readings or sacred song, service at the altar or other ministries—they will first of all try to familiarize themselves with the readings, letting the word echo in their hearts; they will then choose the hymns, possibly prepare a few words of introduction to invite whole-hearted attention, and will write the prayer of the faithful. They will do all this in the way that is most in harmony with the readings, bearing in mind the liturgical

---

and prayers of the Mass, one may consult *La Sainte Messe hier, aujourd'hui et demain*, by Jean-Denis Chalufour, O.S.B. (Petrus a Stella, 2000).

[73] Ibid.

[74] Ibid., §46.

season and seeking to bring out some particular aspect of the rite itself, and they will thus be able to further an understanding of its particular mystagogical significance.

Serving at the altar will be restricted to boys in accordance with tradition, which has always made of this a kind of *pre-seminary*—in any case, a framework particularly suited to awakening priestly vocations. In this sense, it is an excellent means for training them in the *ars celebrandi*.[75] As for girls, one should take care to associate them with other parish ministries.

It remains to say a word about the quality of the *Missals* published for the use of the faithful. We may observe that hidden in the last editions of the daily Missals of Feder or Lefebvre, dating from the early sixties, we find remarkable elements of liturgical formation.[76] This liturgical inspiration is not to be found in contemporary Missals—far from it;

---

[75] Cf. Pope John Paul II's *Letter to Priests for Holy Thursday* of 2004, §6: "In the light of this, dear brother priests, I would ask you, among other initiatives, to *show special care for altar servers*, who represent a kind of 'garden' for priestly vocations. The group of altar servers, under your guidance as part of the parish community, can be given a valuable experience of Christian education and become a kind of pre-seminary."

[76] These Missals had already integrated beforehand the main things requested by the constitution *Sacrosanctum Concilium* by offering the faithful, as an introduction to the ordinary of the Mass in Latin and French, a remarkable catechesis on the meaning of the liturgy. Each Sunday is prefaced with an introduction on the meaning given to the liturgy of the day by the texts of the word of God, with a perspective on the liturgy drawn from other parallel texts from the Bible. Cf. *Missel quotidien et vespéra*, by Dom Gaspar Lefebvre and Canon Émile Osty (Bruges: Éditions de l'apostolat liturgique, 1961): as an epigraph to the introduction to *holy Mass*, we read, "Holy Mass, center of the Church's worship, the inexhaustible and fruitful wellspring of Christian life" (p. 1039). And at the beginning of the "General Order of the Mass", "We see what the Mass represents in Christian life. What should we do, then, to participate in it by giving it its full meaning?" (p. 1041.) This is far from the caricatures that have been smugly circulated by certain craftsmen of the implementation of the liturgical reform.

these include many exegetical notes to help us better appreciate the word of God but are quite impoverished from the mystagogical point of view, as if we had lost the sense of liturgy in favor of a very cerebral interpretation, inherited from the Enlightenment. There is a great deal of work to do in order to form the faithful in the spirit of the liturgy.

Lacking any liturgical formation, a good many celebrants have been unable, in the way they celebrate, to bring out the theological and spiritual wealth of the new Missal, preferring the rites whose deeper meaning they no longer know adaptations and innovations whose banality proves disconcerting. Thus they have deprived the faithful of all wealth—without of course meaning to do so—and have, as it were, sterilized the best intentions of liturgical reform as far as their Christian and spiritual life is concerned. The sole aim of the reform, profiting from the liturgical movement, had been nothing but to make the liturgy once more become the source of an authentically Christian life. What followed was a kind of *regression* and thus, then, a *retrogression*. In much the same way, in fact, as before the liturgical movement, the mass of faithful, having no access to the riches of the Church's liturgy, had to make do with the adulterated devotional prayers with which the pages of their Missals were filled, so today many are deserting an impoverished, cerebral, and dried-up liturgy for forms of devotion with more feeling—private devotions, praise assemblies, and so on—which do have their value but that remain far below the treasure of the liturgy. Others, knowing nothing else, have become used to this cut-rate liturgy and, without agreeing to it, are subjected to a real loss for their spiritual, moral, caritative, and missionary lives.

Hence the urgent need for liturgical formation together with a rediscovery of the authentic meaning of the liturgy, so that it might once more become the source and the summit of the Church's life and so that the faithful might again be able to drink from this stream of living water and be imbued with the "sober intoxication of the Holy Spirit" that characterizes the Roman liturgy.[77]

A REVERENT FEAR

This liturgical formation will also include an education in the feeling of reverent fear before the mystery celebrated in the liturgy, especially in the most holy Eucharist. This is the underlying attitude of man when he is brought into the presence of the mystery of God. Like Moses before the burning bush, we are invited to this *eucharistic wonder* of which John Paul II talked and which is made up of an infinite respect. If God is present in the Eucharist, then we should first of all be filled with a feeling of fear: only God can take the initiative and bring himself near, right to the point of inviting us to enter into his intimacy. We cannot, of ourselves, indiscreetly take possession of such a mystery without a risk of making it banal or of denying its transcendence. This respect is the supreme expression of faith, as suggested by the attitude of the Roman centurion, whose beautiful words have been preserved in the liturgy at the very moment of Communion. This man *did not feel he had the right to approach Jesus* and sent some prominent Jews to speak on his behalf; and then, faced with Christ's solicitude, he shows his awareness of how undeserving he is with a greatness of spirit that extracts the

---

[77] Cf. *Hymnaire latin-français* (Solesmes, 1988), *Hymne des Laudes* (Weeks 1 and 3): "Christus nobis sit cibus, potusque noster sit fides; laeti bibamus sobriam ebrietatem Spiritus (May Christ be our food, may faith be our drink; may we taste with gladness the sober intoxication of the Spirit)."

finest praise from Jesus: "I tell you, not even in Israel have I found such faith."[78]

There is no doubt that if the Council did deepen the social and convivial aspect of the Eucharist, that was often done to the detriment of the real presence of Christ under the appearance of consecrated bread and wine and of the sacrificial nature of the memorial of the Lord's Supper. In emphasizing the concept of a *communal meal*, the sense of the sacred was weakened.[79]

Guided by the sure instinct of faith, the people of God have rediscovered the real presence of the living Jesus in the Eucharist—often in the spheres of influence of the new communities springing from the renewal. There has for some years now been a real infatuation in the life of the Church

[78] Cf. Lk 7:1–10. This page of the Gospel has a lovely lesson on eucharistic education: it suggests, in fact, that all the faithful come to Communion adopt an attitude of great humility, passing by way of the necessity to "examine oneself" in order to "discern the Body of the Lord" (cf. 1 Cor 11:28–29). Pushed to its limits, this justifies the attitude the Church recommends for people who are living in circumstances in objective contradiction to God's holy law; their humble obedience will make it possible for the word of Jesus to do its work of salvation, without any physical contact with Communion: "But say the word, and let my servant be healed. . . . And when those who had been sent returned to the house, they found the slave well." Thus the Church's discipline regarding people who have been divorced and remarried, far from being discriminatory, is in accordance with an attitude of reverent fear which is inherent in the very nature of the Eucharist and defines a law that applies to everyone, whatever their particular situation.

[79] We should read most attentively the long exposition that Joseph Cardinal Ratzinger devotes to "form and content in the eucharistic celebration", in which he shows, starting with the process of the foundation of the Eucharist in the history of the Mass, that the form of eucharistic celebration is not, properly speaking, the *form of a meal*, but rather the form of 'eucharistia', thanksgiving to the Lord, which was uttered at the Last Supper and fulfilled on the Cross, and, thus, the form of a sacrifice: see *The Feast of Faith*, pp. 33–60.

for the practice of eucharistic adoration, which had fallen into disuse immediately after the Council for erroneous reasons.[80] Adoration has awakened respect for the Eucharist in the hearts of the faithful, that reverent fear in the face of the mystery of the living God. Benedict XVI teaches that the "process of mystagogy" should introduce the faithful to this respect "before the infinite majesty of God, who comes to us in the lowliness of the sacramental signs": "I am thinking in general of the importance of gestures and posture, such as kneeling during the central moments of the Eucharistic prayer."[81]

It remains for us to rediscover the sacrificial character of the liturgy. May the motu proprio *Summorum Pontificum* be instrumental in this. I am thinking especially of eucharistic Communion, which represents the summit of that conscious, active, and fruitful participation asked for by the Council. Certainly, Jesus gives himself as food, and that confers on the Eucharist the form of a meal, of a convivial banquet, of a shared union with the Body of Christ. In any case, the old manner of communicating on one's knees before the *holy table*, covered with its tablecloth at the moment of Communion and opportunely extending the altar of sacrifice as the table of the *wedding feast of the Lamb* perhaps signified better the convivial dimension of the Eucharist than cur-

---

[80] Cf. *Sacramentum Caritatis*, §66: "During the early phases of the reform, the inherent relationship between Mass and adoration of the Blessed Sacrament was not always perceived with sufficient clarity. For example, an objection that was widespread at the time argued that the eucharistic bread was given to us not to be looked at, but to be eaten. In the light of the Church's experience of prayer, however, this was seen to be a false dichotomy. As Saint Augustine put it: '*nemo autem illam carnem manducat, nisi prius adoraverit; peccemus non adorando*—no one eats that flesh without first adoring it; we should sin were we not to adore it.'"

[81] Ibid., §65.

rent practice: the priest moved from one guest to another to give them as food the Body of Christ, like Jesus assuring us that he will rise from the table in his Kingdom to serve us.[82] Kneeling, which ought at least to be replaced by some gesture of respect, signifies reverence before the real presence of God in the Host. Similarly, the Communion procession continues to express the fact that following Christ means to enter into a procession that leads him to the Cross and to agree to enter into his obedience to the Father's will, so as to be but one single victim with him;[83] it also means making the effort to pass through the narrow gate[84]—and that gate is his Pasch, that is to say, his Passion, his death, and his Resurrection. We must regain the sense of the Eucharist as a sacrifice through the mystagogy of the rites that express this.

[82] Cf. Lk 12:37.

[83] Cf. Lk 14:27, "Whoever does not bear his own cross and come after me, cannot be my disciple."

[84] Cf. Lk 13:24, "Strive to enter by the narrow door."

III

PARTICIPATION IN THE LITURGY AS AN EXERCISE IN THE *SENSUS FIDEI* AND THE *SENSUS ECCLESIAE*

As Cardinal Ratzinger wrote in March 2003, in his preface to the very fine little book by the English Oratorian Michael Lang on the orientation of liturgical prayer: "To the ordinary churchgoer, the two most obvious effects of the liturgical reform of the Second Vatican Council seem to be the disappearance of Latin and the turning of the altars towards the people. Those who read the relevant texts", the future Pope Benedict XVI continues, "will be astonished to learn that neither is in fact found in the decrees of the Council."[1]

Anyone who has carefully read the constitution *Sacrosanctum Concilium* will have no doubt, on the other hand, that *actuosa participatio* (active participation) constitutes the key concept of the liturgical reform promoted by the Second Vatican Council. In §11, we may read, "Pastors of souls must therefore realize that, when the liturgy is celebrated, something more is required than the mere observation of the laws governing valid and licit celebration; it is their duty also to ensure that the faithful take part fully aware of what they are doing, actively engaged in the rite, and enriched by its effects (*scienter, actuose et fructuose participent*)." Insistence upon active participation recurs in many passages in the constitution, as a leitmotiv and key idea.

[1] Uwe Michael Lang, *Turning towards the Lord: Orientation in Liturgical Prayer* (San Francisco: Ignatius Press, 2004), 9.

1. The Nature of Participation in the Liturgy

a. *An approach through the history of the* liturgical movement

Is this a matter of exterior or interior participation? We have to admit that in actual fact, the main emphasis has been on exterior participation, to the point of those regrettable reductions Benedict XVI mentioned in his exhortation: "Yet we must not overlook the fact that some misunderstanding has occasionally arisen concerning the precise meaning of this participation. It should be made clear that the word 'participation' does not refer to mere external activity during the celebration."[2] Here again, too superficial a reading of the Council's text might lead to mistakes, such as emphasizing above all the role of the faithful as being the newest aspect of the reform: "To promote active participation, the people should be encouraged to take part by means of acclamations, responses, psalmody, antiphons, and songs, as well as by actions, gestures, and bodily attitudes", we read in § 30; and in § 31, "The revision of the liturgical books must carefully attend to the provision of rubrics also for the people's parts."

A study of this concept in the history of the liturgical renewal, however, shows that *active participation* is not a new idea, but one that canonizes, so to speak, a base line of the liturgical movement that was there long before the Council.

---

[2] *Sacramentum Caritatis*, § 52. In his book *The Spirit of the Liturgy*, Joseph Cardinal Ratzinger had already written, "The word was very quickly misunderstood to mean something external, entailing a need for general activity, as if as many people as possible, as often as possible, should be visibly engaged in action" (p. 171).

A quick recap of the history of this idea will in fact help us to understand better its meaning as used by the Council. We find it in the nineteenth century in the *first liturgical movement*'s preoccupation with associating the faithful with the sacred rites through congregational singing.

Yet it was especially Saint Pius X's 1903 motu proprio *Tra le Sollecitudini* that promoted active participation to the rank of operative concept of liturgical renewal: "Filled as We are with a most ardent desire to see the true Christian spirit flourish in every respect and be preserved by all the faithful, We deem it necessary to provide before anything else for the sanctity and dignity of the temple in which the faithful assemble for no other object than that of acquiring this spirit from its *foremost and indispensable font*, which is the *active participation* in the most holy mysteries and in the public and solemn prayer of the Church." It is worthy of note that this passage by Saint Pius X is repeated, almost literally (yet without any explicit reference), in §14 of *Sacrosanctum Concilium*: "In the restoration and promotion of the sacred liturgy, this full and active participation by all the people is the aim to be considered before all else; for it is *the primary and indispensable source* from which the faithful are to derive *the true Christian spirit*." We can clearly see that in the mind of Saint Pius X this is first and foremost a matter of participating in the mystery of the Eucharist, made more accessible by frequent Communion and, in the second place, by attention to the congregational hymns, so that certain kinds of lyrics should no longer distract them from the essence of the mystery. In the same way, does not the constitution *Sacrosanctum Concilium* recommend sacramental Communion as "perfectior Missae participatio" (§55), and does it not stress singing by the faithful as the supreme expression of this active participation (cf. §§30, 114)?

Along the lines suggested by Saint Pius X, the liturgical movement, in starting with eucharistic Communion, in its dual aspect—interior, as *contact with the mystery*, and ritual, as reception of the Sacrament—would continue in the direction of an *exteriorization* of the concept of *active participation* by emphasizing the requisite understanding of the liturgical texts, then by inspiring initiatives that affected the external form of worship, through involving the faithful in singing and in gestures.

b. A participation that is both internal and external

For all that, it is still clear what the Council wished: it is a matter, as we can read in §19 of *Sacrosanctum Concilium*, of instructing the faithful in "inward and external participation". How, indeed, could one dissociate these two aspects of participation, since they represent the two faces of one and the same reality?

Everything depends on the nature of the liturgical action in which we are invited to participate in an active way: in fact, this participation, as we read in §14, "is demanded by the very nature of the liturgy". Here, the Council's teaching is summarized in the *Compendium of the Catechism of the Catholic Church* as follows: "The liturgy is the celebration of the mystery of Christ and in particular his paschal mystery" (§218). Thus, the *actio* in which we are called to participate is the very *actio* of Christ, continued by his Body which is the Church, and it is divine before becoming ours; it is the very work of our redemption which is being effected, precisely through the Paschal Mystery of Christ, made present in the Church's liturgy. Thus we can understand the request so frequently expressed by the postconciliar Magisterium, especially when faced with the abuses to which the implementation of the liturgical reform has often led, that we *rediscover the meaning of the mystery*.

Because man, who is called to participate in the liturgy as a celebration of the mystery of our redemption, is of a bodily and social nature, active participation will necessarily be carried out through external activity. But, in accordance with the adage "agere sequitur esse", external activity, even sacred actions, are rooted in an act that is of the order of being, as a kind of active power, and is none other than the participation in the divine nature, without which the liturgical action would not be proportionate to its object. This is what Pope John Paul II concluded, in the text we have quoted above, "As the tradition of the venerable Eastern Churches also clearly emphasizes, it is through the liturgy that the faithful enter into communion with the Most Holy Trinity and experience their sharing in the divine nature as a gift of grace."[3]

Thus there is no contradiction between external and internal participation in the liturgy. Any truly human action, as Saint Thomas tells us, is made up of an internal act and an external act:[4] these are contained within each other and constitute one and the same reality, just as the body and the soul are but one single person, and as matter and form contribute to the unity of all created reality, in accordance with the principle of hylomorphism. And it is obviously in this sense that we must understand the aim of the Council.

Moreover, §11 of *Sacrosanctum Concilium* introduces this emphasis on conscious, active, and fruitful participation

---

[3] *Ecclesia in Europa*, §70.
[4] Cf. *Summa Theologiae* Ia–IIae, q. 18, a. 6.

with these words: "But in order that the liturgy may be able to produce its full effects, it is necessary that the faithful come to it with proper dispositions, that their minds should be attuned to their voices, and that they should co-operate with divine grace lest they receive it in vain."

2. The Theological Basis of Active Participation[5]

Pope Pius XII, with the encyclical *Mediator Dei*, directly prepared the way for the Council's reform by emphasizing the theological basis of participation; it was a matter of what the Second Vatican Council was to call the *common priesthood of all believers*: "By the waters of baptism, as by common right, Christians are made members of the Mystical Body of Christ the Priest, and by the 'character' which is imprinted on their souls, they are appointed to give worship to God. Thus they participate, according to their condition, in the priesthood of Christ" (§88). Having established this, Pope Pius XII, in a very daring way, describes the participation of the faithful in the liturgy as a *co-offering* of the sacrifice by all the faithful together with the priest, and not only "by the hands of the priest" (§92), since it is the whole Church that presents the victim through Christ and his minister. We then comprehend that the subject in the liturgy is the Church as the Mystical Body of Christ, in which Christ makes present his work of redemption. The encyclical then invites the faithful to offer themselves in union with the sacrifice of Christ and thus render by the gift of their whole

[5] This section is indebted to the dissertation for the canonical license in theology [approximate equivalent of Master's degree—TRANS.] of Thomas Diradourian, C.S.M., *La liturgie des heures, modèle, témoin et promoteur de la participation liturgique* (Fribourg, 2005).

lives a spiritual worship to God, in the sense in which Saint Paul speaks of this.[6] Then, as a consequence, there are directions on the concrete ways, in pastoral terms, of promoting the participation of the faithful in the sacred ceremonies.

This teaching in the encyclical *Mediator Dei* governs the whole of the Second Vatican Council's exposition on the common priesthood of the faithful. This may be judged by the following extracts from the dogmatic constitution *Lumen Gentium*: "Though they differ from one another in essence and not only in degree, the common priesthood of the faithful and the ministerial or hierarchical priesthood are nonetheless interrelated: each of them in its own special way is a participation in the one priesthood of Christ," we read in §10; and in §11, "Incorporated in the Church through baptism, the faithful are destined by the baptismal character for the worship of the Christian religion. . . . Taking part in the eucharistic sacrifice, which is the fount and apex of the whole Christian life, they offer the Divine Victim to God, and offer themselves along with It."

Pius XII's teaching is still more explicit in §48 of *Sacrosanctum Concilium*, in connection with the active participation of the faithful in the *mysterium fidei* that is the eucharistic sacrifice of the Body and Blood of the Lord: "By offering the Immaculate Victim," it says, "not only through the hands of the priest, but also with him, they should learn also to offer themselves; through Christ the Mediator, they should be drawn day by day into ever more perfect union with God and with each other."

Three principles explain the theological meaning of this participation:

---

[6] Cf. Rom 12:1.

a. Entrance into the mystery

It is not a matter of the liturgy creating the conditions for contact with the mystery, but of welcoming its presence, of celebrating its presence through the rite of the Eucharist that the Lord himself instituted. It is thus a matter of participating, in the sense of *sharing* in the Paschal Mystery of Christ, which is made present in a real sense in the liturgy. Before being the celebration of the mystery, then, the liturgy is the very mystery that is being celebrated! Thus we come back to John Paul II's insistent urging, in the apostolic exhortation *Ecclesia in Europa*, of the task of "rediscovering the sense of 'mystery'; in renewing liturgical celebrations so that they can be more eloquent signs of the presence of Christ the Lord" (§69). Thus, participation will merely be the result, in pastoral terms, of making the mystery present through the liturgy: since the mystery is present, it is necessary to be present to it! Hence the concept of conscious participation —conscious of the mystery that is thus made present and that is prior to the celebration itself.

b. The corporate subject of the participation

If it is by virtue of baptism, which makes them participants in the priesthood of Christ, that the faithful are called to take an active part in the liturgy, it is through the hands of the priests that they are able to do so. In other words, seen from this aspect, the ministerial priesthood is ordered to the very exercise of the common priesthood of the faithful. This stresses the organic character of the active participation of the faithful: as *Lumen Gentium* says: "All take part in this liturgical service, not indeed, all in the same way but each in that way which is proper to himself" (§11).

Moreover, *Sacrosanctum Concilium* emphasizes not only the organic nature of the participation, but also its communal aspect. For it is the Church that is the subject of the liturgy. If each person takes part in the liturgy through his personal integration into the Church, as a member of the Mystical Body of Christ, delegated to share, each in his own way, in the worship celebrated by the whole Christ, then it is necessary to explain that the faithful, taken as a whole, are all but one in Christ, since the grace received individually is the life of one single body. In virtue of this communion of grace, the unity of the assembly constituted by the faithful is not in the first instance psychological nor sociological; it is ontological and thus precedes the participation of each in the liturgy. This is how *Sacrosanctum Concilium* puts it: "Liturgical services are not private functions, but are celebrations of the Church, which is the 'sacrament of unity', namely, the holy people united and ordered under their bishops." (§26) That is why they make manifest the whole body of the Church.

c. Integration into the twofold mediation

Because the liturgy is essentially "an action of Christ the priest",[7] through which "the sanctification of men in Christ and the glorification of God . . . is achieved in the most efficacious possible way",[8] both the descending and ascending dimension of Christ's mediation, rendered present in the liturgy, is emphasized.

Thus there is no opposition between these two dimensions; rather, there is a precise balance that finds its source in the very work of Christ the mediator. In other words, the

---

[7] *Sacrosanctum Concilium*, §7.
[8] Ibid., §10.

participation of the faithful will be made with an attitude that is both receptive and active: receptive of the graces and blessings that descend from on high and that can be given only at the Lord's initiative; and active in the community of faithful who are sending up the offering themselves so as to unite it with Christ's offering. Here again, we see that it is in the person of Christ and his sacrificial offering, made present in the sacrament of the Eucharist, that the sanctification and glorification are made one. And thus active participation necessarily has a *liturgical form* defined by the Church's Magisterium, which does not, for all that, exclude any participation incarnate in space and time. A precise balance that is inherent in the liturgical action and that may not be left to the whim of a "liturgical team"!

3. Participation as an Exercise of the *Sensus Fidei*

a. The ambiguities of active participation

If we look closely at the Council's recommendations about *participatio actuosa*, we can clearly see that external activities are particularly emphasized. Three pastoral principles govern even this exterior participation.

There is, first of all, the organization of the liturgy, that is to say, the distribution of roles. In §50 of *Sacrosanctum Concilium* we read, "The rite of the Mass is to be revised in such a way that the intrinsic nature and purpose of its several parts . . . may be more clearly manifested."[9] Then there is the question of intelligibility: in §34, the Council Fathers emphasize the *noble simplicity* of the rites, the *trans-*

---

[9] See also §28.

parency of the signs, and the understanding of the texts and signs that facilitate comprehension. Finally, there is the matter of the communal nature of the liturgical action, which prevails over any individual or private celebration.[10]

It is necessary to observe that unless the living connection between exterior and interior participation is clearly enough established, then these pastoral principles can lead to a mistaken conception of liturgy that will be expressed in terms of an excessive dramatization of the roles, a reductive cerebralization of the rites, and an improper self-celebration on the part of the assembly.

We have to say that "the principal schools of sociology 'available' when the Council opened were positivist, empiricist, or functionalist."[11] On the basis of presuppositions deriving more from rationalist Enlightenment philosophy than from the Church's great theological tradition, people sought to achieve simplicity, wishing to reconnect with the practices of the early Church; they refused a priori, however, to see in the increasing ritual complexity, down the centuries, an enrichment of the liturgy that might well stem from an ever more profound experience by the subject-Church of the mystery of Christ. In the same way, they started from the principle that the more intelligible a rite is, the more it gives rise to a profound assent, whereas contemporary sociologists affirm that, on the contrary, a certain opacity is requisite in any symbolic act. And if, in the name of distributing the roles, we witness an excessive personalization, or even a dramatization of each person's role, this often occurs to the detriment of the manifestation of the person of Christ himself, who should have the central place in the liturgy.

---

[10] Cf. §27.

[11] Aidan Nichols, O.P., *Looking at the Liturgy: A Critical View of Its Contemporary Form* (San Francisco: Ignatius Press, 1996), p. 57.

The result has very often been, in liturgical celebrations, a most unfortunate impoverishment of the sense of faith, even a harmful flattening of the mystery.

The desiccated state of the liturgy resulting in this way from too rationalistic a conception of active participation has in reaction paradoxically given rise to a kind of liturgical romanticism, in which the excessive cerebralization gives way to an exaggerated sentimentality, increased by that other request made by some modern liturgists to create warm and living communities that reduce the liturgy to a celebration in the sense of a party or entertainment, in relation to the frequently heavy trials of life.[12]

b. A theological action rooted in the sensus fidei

The only way to avoid an exaggeration of the pastoral principles laid down by the Council for the guidance of external participation—an exaggeration due to too close an association with questionable sociological presuppositions—is in fact to go back to the very source of this participation. For in the final analysis, the active participation that the Council promotes resides precisely in that association between interior and exterior participation. The fact is that before being a role played by the celebrant or the faithful, participation is a theological action.

What is involved in the liturgy first of all is not reason or emotion but faith—and not primarily as an act, but as a virtue, as a habitual attitude: as the *sensus fidei*. The constitution *Lumen Gentium*, in §12, recalled the existence of this

---

[12] Cardinal Ratzinger has explained this concept of celebration in the liturgy and the danger it runs of getting out of control in *The Feast of Faith*, trans. Graham Harrison (San Francisco: Ignatius Press, 1986), pp. 62–75.

very *sensus fidei*, the supernatural sense of faith, and defined it as follows:

> The entire body of the faithful, anointed as they are by the Holy One (cf. 1 Jn. 2:20, 27), cannot err in matters of belief. They manifest this special property by means of the whole people's supernatural discernment in matters of faith [*sensus fidei*] when "from the Bishops down to the last of the lay faithful" they show universal agreement [*consensus*] in matters of faith and morals. That discernment in matters of faith is aroused and sustained by the Spirit of truth. It is exercised under the guidance of the sacred teaching authority, in faithful and respectful obedience to which the people of God accepts that which is not just the word of men but truly the word of God (cf. 1 Thess. 2, 13). Through it, the people of God adheres unwaveringly to the faith given once and for all to the saints (cf. Jud. 3), penetrates it more deeply with right thinking, and applies it more fully in its life.

The Council connects this supernatural sense of faith, which is brought to life by the Holy Spirit and educated by the holy Magisterium, to a *"consensus"*. This term, analyzed by Saint Thomas Aquinas in his study of human action,[13] means more than the assent of the intellect; it is laden with a whole weight of affectivity—obviously, I am talking about profound affectivity, that of the will that is spontaneously attracted by good, *"good that is in accordance with reason"*, the only thing that can fulfill the deepest longings of the heart and in which the will, as spiritual appetite, instinctively finds pleasure. This does not derive from a *consensus* among men, as if it were subject to universal suffrage. We ought not to confuse the *sensus fidei* with the *sensus fidelium*: a majority of

---

[13] Cf. *Summa Theologiae*, Ia–IIae, q. 15.

the faithful may well, in a given context, be in contradiction to the *sensus fidei* and may respond albeit unconsciously, more to the pressures of environment or custom than to the voice of God that sounds in the depths of the heart and that cannot be in contradiction with the teaching of the holy Magisterium. This is what makes it so difficult for many of the faithful, led into error by a certain implementation of the reform, to accept the motu proprio's invitation to rediscover the sacredness of the liturgy.

So as not to be reduced to a sensitivity to fashion, the *sensus fidelium* must express the *sensus fidei*, which for its own part is "aroused and sustained by the Spirit of truth". The *sensus fidei*, which comes from God, who is truth, having come down through the gift of theological faith into our intellect in order to draw our whole being to himself: when our intellect assents to the truth of faith, it does so at the impulse of the will, which mysteriously perceives this truth as the good that fulfils the person as a whole, of which the will is in fact the appetite.

We can thus understand how the *supernatural sense of faith* altogether precedes explicit assent to a clearly formulated faith and is in a certain sense far richer. It refers to the spontaneous assent by the faithful to the mystery of God, in virtue of a kind of suitable proportioning of the intellect and hearts of the believers to the mystery of God—a process that is itself mysterious and, thus, in a sense inexpressible, incapable of formulation. This is a knowledge on the basis of *connaturality*, born of a profound experience of divinity that is wholly interior, wholly invisible. It is understandable why, when the faithful—even a majority of them, if it were possible—do not assent to the truths of faith taught by the Magisterium of the Church, or to the demands of evangelical morality recalled by that same Magisterium for our time, then they do not react at the same profound level attained by the *sensus fidei*, but are more obedient to their more or less wounded psychology or their feelings . . . , and there is nothing more easily manipulated than feelings.

c. The liturgy as an exercise of the sensus fidei

In the first place, then, the liturgy must put the faithful in touch with the very mystery of the presence of God, must make possible that profound experience which is that of faith, by appealing in the first instance to the *sensus fidei*, aroused and sustained by the Spirit of truth within us, right from the day of our baptism, and ought not to appeal first to the *intellectus fidei* or to our feelings.

So we can understand why the liturgy, in wanting to put us in touch with the very mystery of Christ the Lord, who "dwells in our hearts through faith", as Saint Paul says,[14] ought not to be intelligible in the first instance, but should, on the contrary, retain a certain opacity so as to facilitate that experience of the divine which one will then be better able to articulate as adequately as possible, but always in a way that falls short of the mystery, through the confession of faith and the practice of the Christian life.

This is why the Council did not foresee that the liturgy would be entirely in the vernacular. In this sense, far from being obstacles to active participation, celebrating Mass *toward the Lord* rather than *toward the people*, the use of Latin—which the Council did not recommend abandoning entirely, despite certain deep-rooted prejudices (see § 36)—and the use of Gregorian chant, which *Sacrosanctum Concilium* referred to as "specially suited to the Roman liturgy", even observing that it should "be given pride of place" (§ 116), will on the

---

[14] Cf. Eph 3:17.

contrary help toward authentic participation in the liturgy, which is above all a divine action, the action of the Lord himself, and thus transcendent.

Thus, for example, there is nothing ideological or nostalgic in a preference for Latin and Gregorian chant; it is first and foremost the fruit of an experience of the liturgy as a communal celebration of faith: not in the first instance a subjective faith, such as is necessarily embodied in a way of life influenced by the history of a person or a family, with its wealth and its wounds, but the faith of the universal Church, in which everyone is united through what is beyond himself and which the Second Vatican Council did in fact call the *sensus fidei*, the supernatural sense of faith, which places each believer instinctively on the same level with, in connaturality with, in assent with the mystery revealed by God in Scripture, as it is handed down by the holy Magisterium and celebrated in the liturgy of the Church. Thus the *sensus fidei* and the *sensus Ecclesiae* are intrinsically united. There is no doubt, then, that Gregorian chant will help us return to the properly contemplative dimension of the liturgy . . . not to mention that it will allow us to grow in communion with the universal Church, putting us in touch in a mysterious way with the values of faith and holiness of the Church of all times and all places, the Church whose heart beats at Rome.

CONCLUSION

THE OPEN PATH TO A NEW STAGE
OF THE LITURGICAL MOVEMENT

The motu proprio *Summorum Pontificum*, then, certainly is a liturgical event. It does not aim to *reestablish* the old Missal—which has in any case never been abrogated and ought never to have been forbidden. But it is trying to invite pastors and faithful to take another look at the way they celebrate the liturgy according to the ordinary form of the Roman rite: this is what is really at stake. Indeed, in asserting that "there is no contradiction between the two editions of the *Missale Romanum*", called even to "be mutually enriching", and in expressing the wish that the Missal of Paul VI be celebrated "with great reverence in harmony with the liturgical directives", Benedict XVI is hoping to lessen the distance that currently exists between the two forms of usage of the Roman rite, particularly in the art of celebration. Furthermore, in emphasizing *the growth and progress* that have always characterized the history of the Latin liturgy, he is opening the path to subsequent developments, on condition that we fight against a certain *break with tradition*. So above and beyond a fatherly hand extended to those children of the Church attached to the old form of the Roman rite, turbulent and undisciplined but also often unjustly treated as they sometimes may be, the motu proprio constitutes an invitation to everyone to rediscover the authentic meaning of the liturgy. It marks a new stage, whose importance should not be underestimated, in the recent history of the liturgy and, thus, in the homogenous and unbroken progress of the liturgical movement, the work of which, started by Saint Pius X and encouraged by Pius XII, can be carried forward. And who knows whether, when peace reigns once more, a *reform of the reform* will not make its appearance? For the moment, the motu proprio makes an urgent appeal to look again at the principles of the Second Vatican Council's liturgical reform, with humility enough to acknowledge the mistakes of interpretation and implementation made in their regard, especially as concerns the conscious, active, and fruitful participation of the faithful in the liturgical action.

I have in fact tried to show how *participatio actuosa* was indeed the key concept in the liturgical reform promoted by the Second Vatican Council, but in a sense consistent with the tradition of the Church, on condition that the exterior participation being promoted by the reform should indeed be the expression of an inner participation, experienced as a theological action. As is suggested by Jesus' reply to the audacious request from the sons of Zebedee,[1] the important thing is not to play some role or strive to get a place of honor, but in fact to drink from the cup that Jesus was going to drink and to be baptized with the baptism with which he had to be baptized, that is to say, to enter into Christ's Paschal Mystery through faith and love. It is at this existential level that *participatio actuosa* is situated, as an exercise in the *sensus fidei*.

If the implementation of the liturgical reform had been more faithful to the spirit and pastoral recommendations of the constitution *Sacrosanctum Concilium*, then no doubt many

[1] Cf. Mt 20:20ff.

misunderstandings, many tensions, many divisions, many exclusions would have been avoided. The commotion in France that surrounds the gestures that Benedict XVI, like his revered predecessor, the Servant of God John Paul II has increasingly made toward the faithful attached to what is known as the liturgy of Saint Pius V, shows that these tensions are still very present, at least among some who are disappointed by the "springtime in the Church" proclaimed forty years ago. It is at any rate clear that the younger clergy, and likewise the young families of the *John Paul II generation*, so many of whom we find both in the new realities of the postconciliar Church—as varied as the Community of Saint John, the Community of Saint Martin, and the ecclesial movements springing from the charismatic renewal, to name but a few—and also in the traditionalist groups of faithful and institutes of priests, whose average age is fairly low, consider those tensions and exclusions as a rearguard action. What in fact they all have in common is that, in a healthy reaction to the ideology of a *secular Christianity*, the arrival of which was celebrated in the sixties, they are trying to experience the primacy of grace and are often committed to promoting a *spirituality of communion* in the field.

In that sense, Pope Benedict XVI is giving us a marvelous pastoral lesson. What is "pastoral", in fact, but the art of the good shepherd who "knows his sheep, and his sheep know him" and who "lays down his life for the sheep",[2] sparing no pains to bring all his children together in unity, like a good family father. The liturgy, the *source and the summit of the life and mission of the Church*, must cease to be the psychological locus of division and exclusion. It must become once more

[2] Cf. Jn 10.

the theological and spiritual locus of communion. Differences connected with history or with the specific charisms of one or another group, far from threatening divisions, can on the contrary become promises of communion, precisely through the mutual enrichment they bring about. It is not, for all that, a matter of acceding to various *sensibilities*, as is often said, since belonging to the Church is not a matter of sensibility but of *sensus fidei* and of charisms—that is, of the free gifts of the Holy Spirit with a view to the good of the Body as a whole, and intended to build up the unity of the Church that gives to everyone the gift of *sentire cum Ecclesia*, as Saint Ignatius says in his Exercises. That same § 12 in *Lumen Gentium* that emphasized the importance of the *sensus fidei* of God's people did in addition praise the multiplicity of charisms with which the Holy Spirit adorns the Church with a view to everyone's good.

May the establishment of the liturgical peace desired by the Holy Father contribute to the growth of communion within the Church. I am convinced that this motu proprio can help toward the achievement of the hope expressed in his time by Joseph Cardinal Ratzinger: "A renewal of liturgical awareness, a liturgical reconciliation that again recognizes the unity of the history of the liturgy and that understands Vatican II, not as a breach, but as a stage of development: these things are urgently needed for the life of the Church. . . . That is why we need a new Liturgical Movement, which will call to life the real heritage of the Second Vatican Council."[3] This is an important challenge that Benedict XVI seems particularly set to accept.

---

[3] Joseph Ratzinger, *Milestones: Memoirs 1927–1977*, trans. Erasmo Leiva-Merikakis (San Francisco: Ignatius Press, 1998), pp. 148–49.

So, we must pray for the Holy Father. Is that not what he so insistently asked of the faithful assembled in Saint Peter's Square at the inauguration of this pontificate: "Pray for me, that I may not flee for fear of the wolves."[4]

Toulon, September 14, 2007
on the Feast of the Glorious Cross

---

[4] Homily of April 24, 2005.

Apostolic Letter in the Form of
"Motu Proprio" Summorum Pontificum

Up to our own times, it has been the constant concern of supreme pontiffs to ensure that the Church of Christ offers a worthy ritual to the Divine Majesty, "to the praise and glory of His name" and "to the benefit of all His Holy Church".

Since time immemorial it has been necessary—as it is also for the future—to maintain the principle according to which "each particular Church must concur with the universal Church, not only as regards the doctrine of the faith and the sacramental signs, but also as regards the usages universally accepted by uninterrupted apostolic tradition, which must be observed not only to avoid errors but also to transmit the integrity of the faith, because the Church's law of prayer corresponds to her law of faith."[1]

Among the pontiffs who showed that requisite concern, particularly outstanding is the name of Saint Gregory the Great, who made every effort to ensure that the new peoples of Europe received both the Catholic faith and the treasures of worship and culture that had been accumulated by the Romans in preceding centuries. He commanded that the

Unofficial translation from the Vatican Information Service.

[1] *General Instruction of the Roman Missal*, 3rd ed. (2002), no. 397.

form of the sacred liturgy as celebrated in Rome (concerning both the Sacrifice of Mass and the Divine Office) be conserved. He took great concern to ensure the dissemination of monks and nuns who, following the Rule of Saint Benedict, together with the announcement of the Gospel illustrated with their lives the wise provision of their Rule that "nothing should be placed before the work of God." In this way the sacred liturgy, celebrated according to the Roman use, enriched not only the faith and piety but also the culture of many peoples. It is known, in fact, that the Latin liturgy of the Church in its various forms, in each century of the Christian era, has been a spur to the spiritual life of many saints, has reinforced many peoples in the virtue of religion and fecundated their piety.

Many other Roman pontiffs, in the course of the centuries, showed particular solicitude in ensuring that the sacred liturgy accomplished this task more effectively. Outstanding among them is Saint Pius V, who, sustained by great pastoral zeal and following the exhortations of the Council of Trent, renewed the entire liturgy of the Church, oversaw the publication of liturgical books, amended and "renewed in accordance with the norms of the Fathers", and provided them for the use of the Latin Church.

One of the liturgical books of the Roman rite is the Roman Missal, which developed in the city of Rome and, with the passing of the centuries, little by little took forms very similar to that it has had in recent times.

"It was towards this same goal that succeeding Roman Pontiffs directed their energies during the subsequent centuries in order to ensure that the rites and liturgical books were brought up to date and when necessary clarified. From the beginning of this century they undertook a more general reform."[2] Thus our predecessors Clement VIII, Urban VIII, Saint Pius X,[3] Benedict XV, Pius XII, and Blessed John XXIII all played a part.

In more recent times, Vatican Council II expressed a desire that the respectful reverence due to divine worship should be renewed and adapted to the needs of our time. Moved by this desire, our predecessor, the Supreme Pontiff Paul VI, approved, in 1970, reformed, and partly renewed liturgical books for the Latin Church. These, translated into the various languages of the world, were willingly accepted by bishops, priests, and faithful. John Paul II amended the third typical edition of the Roman Missal. Thus Roman pontiffs have operated to ensure that "this kind of liturgical edifice . . . should again appear resplendent for its dignity and harmony."[4]

But in some regions, no small numbers of faithful adhered and continue to adhere with great love and affection to the earlier liturgical forms. These had so deeply marked their culture and their spirit that in 1984 the Supreme Pontiff John Paul II, moved by a concern for the pastoral care of these faithful, with the special indult "Quattuor abhinc annos", issued by the Congregation for Divine Worship, granted permission to use the Roman Missal published by Blessed John XXIII in the year 1962. Later, in the year 1988, John Paul II with the Apostolic Letter given as Motu Proprio, "*Ecclesia Dei*", exhorted bishops to make generous use

---

[2] John Paul II, apostolic letter *Vicesimus quintus annus*, December 4, 1988, 3: *AAS* 81 (1989), 899.

[3] Ibid.

[4] Saint Pius X, apostolic letter motu proprio data *Abhinc duos annos*, October 23, 1913: *AAS* 5 (1913), 449–50; cf. John Paul II, apostolic letter *Vicesimus quintus annus*, no. 3: *AAS* 81 (1989), 899.

of this power in favor of all the faithful who so desired.

Following the insistent prayers of these faithful, long deliberated upon by our predecessor John Paul II, and after having listened to the views of the Cardinal Fathers of the Consistory of 22 March 2006, having reflected deeply upon all aspects of the question, invoked the Holy Spirit, and trusting in the help of God, with these Apostolic Letters we establish the following:

ART. 1. The Roman Missal promulgated by Paul VI is the ordinary expression of the "Lex orandi" (Law of prayer) of the Catholic Church of the Latin rite. Nonetheless, the Roman Missal promulgated by Saint Pius V and reissued by Bl. John XXIII is to be considered as an extraordinary expression of that same "Lex orandi", and must be given due honor for its venerable and ancient usage. These two expressions of the Church's Lex orandi will in no way lead to a division in the Church's "Lex credendi" (Law of belief). They are, in fact, two usages of the one Roman rite.

It is, therefore, permissible to celebrate the Sacrifice of the Mass following the typical edition of the Roman Missal promulgated by Bl. John XXIII in 1962 and never abrogated, as an extraordinary form of the Liturgy of the Church. The conditions for the use of this Missal as laid down by earlier documents, "Quattuor abhinc annos" and "Ecclesia Dei", are substituted as follows:

ART. 2. In Masses celebrated without the people, each Catholic priest of the Latin rite, whether secular or regular, may use the Roman Missal published by Bl. Pope John XXIII in 1962 or the Roman Missal promulgated by Pope Paul VI in 1970, and may do so on any day with the exception of the Easter Triduum. For such celebrations, with either one

Missal or the other, the priest has no need for permission from the Apostolic See or from his Ordinary.

ART. 3. Communities of Institutes of consecrated life and of Societies of apostolic life, of either pontifical or diocesan right, wishing to celebrate Mass in accordance with the edition of the Roman Missal promulgated in 1962, for conventual or "community" celebration in their oratories, may do so. If an individual community or an entire Institute or Society wishes to undertake such celebrations often, habitually, or permanently, the decision must be taken by the Superiors Major, in accordance with the law and following their own specific decrees and statues.

ART. 4. Celebrations of Mass as mentioned above in art. 2 may—observing all the norms of law—also be attended by faithful who, of their own free will, ask to be admitted.

ART. 5. §1. In parishes, where there is a stable group of faithful who adhere to the earlier liturgical tradition, the pastor should willingly accept their requests to celebrate the Mass according to the rite of the Roman Missal published in 1962 and ensure that the welfare of these faithful harmonizes with the ordinary pastoral care of the parish, under the guidance of the bishop in accordance with canon 392, avoiding discord and favoring the unity of the whole Church.

§2. Celebration in accordance with the Missal of Bl. John XXIII may take place on working days; while on Sundays and feast days one such celebration may also be held.

§3. For faithful and priests who request it, the pastor should also allow celebrations in this extraordinary form for special circumstances such as marriages, funerals, or occasional celebrations, e.g., pilgrimages.

§4. Priests who use the Missal of Bl. John XXIII must be qualified to do so and not juridically impeded.

§5. In churches that are not parish or conventual churches, it is the duty of the Rector of the church to grant the above permission.

ART. 6. In Masses celebrated in the presence of the people in accordance with the Missal of Bl. John XXIII, the readings may be given in the vernacular, using editions recognized by the Apostolic See.

ART. 7. If a group of lay faithful, as mentioned in art. 5 §1, has not obtained satisfaction to their requests from the pastor, they should inform the diocesan bishop. The bishop is strongly requested to satisfy their wishes. If he cannot arrange for such celebration to take place, the matter should be referred to the Pontifical Commission "Ecclesia Dei".

ART. 8. A bishop who, desirous of satisfying such requests, but who for various reasons is unable to do so, may refer the problem to the Commission "Ecclesia Dei" to obtain counsel and assistance.

ART. 9. §1. The pastor, having attentively examined all aspects, may also grant permission to use the earlier ritual for the administration of the Sacraments of Baptism, Marriage, Penance, and the Anointing of the Sick, if the good of souls would seem to require it.

§2. Ordinaries are given the right to celebrate the Sacrament of Confirmation using the earlier Roman Pontifical, if the good of souls would seem to require it.

§3. Clerics ordained "in sacris constitutis" may use the Roman Breviary promulgated by Bl. John XXIII in 1962.

ART. 10. The ordinary of a particular place, if he feels it appropriate, may erect a personal parish in accordance with can. 518 for celebrations following the ancient form of the Roman rite, or appoint a chaplain, while observing all the norms of law.

ART. 11. The Pontifical Commission "Ecclesia Dei", erected by John Paul II in 1988,[5] continues to exercise its function.
    Said Commission will have the form, duties, and norms that the Roman Pontiff wishes to assign it.

ART. 12. This Commission, apart from the powers it enjoys, will exercise the authority of the Holy See, supervising the observance and application of these dispositions.

We order that everything We have established with these Apostolic Letters issued as Motu Proprio be considered as "established and decreed", and to be observed from 14 September of this year, Feast of the Exaltation of the Cross, whatever there may be to the contrary.

> *From Rome, at Saint Peter's, 7 July 2007, third year of Our Pontificate.*

BENEDICT XVI

---

[5] Cf. John Paul II, apostolic letter motu proprio data *Ecclesia Dei*, July 2, 1988, no. 6: *AAS* 80 (1988), 1498.

Letter of His Holiness Benedict XVI to the Bishops on the Occasion of the Publication of the Apostolic Letter "Motu Proprio Data" Summorum Pontificum on the Use of the Roman Liturgy Prior to the Reform of 1970

My dear Brother Bishops,

With great trust and hope, I am consigning to you as Pastors the text of a new Apostolic Letter "Motu Proprio data" on the use of the Roman liturgy prior to the reform of 1970. The document is the fruit of much reflection, numerous consultations, and prayer.

News reports and judgments made without sufficient information have created no little confusion. There have been very divergent reactions, ranging from joyful acceptance to harsh opposition, about a plan whose contents were in reality unknown.

This document was most directly opposed on account of two fears, which I would like to address somewhat more closely in this letter.

In the first place, there is the fear that the document detracts from the authority of the Second Vatican Council, one of whose essential decisions—the liturgical reform—is being called into question.

This fear is unfounded. In this regard, it must first be said that the Missal published by Paul VI and then republished in two subsequent editions by John Paul II obviously is and continues to be the normal Form—the *Forma ordinaria*—of the eucharistic liturgy. The last version of the *Missale Romanum* prior to the Council, which was published with the authority of Pope John XXIII in 1962 and used during the Council, will now be able to be used as a *Forma extraordinaria* of the liturgical celebration. It is not appropriate to speak of these two versions of the Roman Missal as if they were "two Rites". Rather, it is a matter of a twofold use of one and the same rite.

As for the use of the 1962 Missal as a *Forma extraordinaria* of the liturgy of the Mass, I would like to draw attention to the fact that this Missal was never juridically abrogated and, consequently, in principle, was always permitted. At the time of the introduction of the new Missal, it did not seem necessary to issue specific norms for the possible use of the earlier Missal. Probably it was thought that it would be a matter of a few individual cases which would be resolved, case by case, on the local level. Afterwards, however, it soon became apparent that a good number of people remained strongly attached to this usage of the Roman Rite, which had been familiar to them from childhood. This was especially the case in countries where the liturgical movement had provided many people with a notable liturgical formation and a deep, personal familiarity with the earlier Form of the liturgical celebration. We all know that, in the movement led by Archbishop Lefebvre, fidelity to the old Missal became an external mark of identity; the reasons for the break which arose over this, however, were at a deeper level. Many people who clearly accepted the binding character of the Second Vatican Council, and were faithful to the Pope and the Bishops, nonetheless also desired to recover the form of the sacred liturgy that was dear to them.

This occurred above all because in many places celebrations were not faithful to the prescriptions of the new Missal, but the latter actually was understood as authorizing or even requiring creativity, which frequently led to deformations of the liturgy which were hard to bear. I am speaking from experience, since I too lived through that period with all its hopes and its confusion. And I have seen how arbitrary deformations of the liturgy caused deep pain to individuals totally rooted in the faith of the Church.

Pope John Paul II thus felt obliged to provide, in his Motu Proprio *Ecclesia Dei* (2 July 1988), guidelines for the use of the 1962 Missal; that document, however, did not contain detailed prescriptions but appealed in a general way to the generous response of Bishops towards the "legitimate aspirations" of those members of the faithful who requested this usage of the Roman Rite. At the time, the Pope primarily wanted to assist the Society of Saint Pius X to recover full unity with the Successor of Peter and sought to heal a wound experienced ever more painfully. Unfortunately this reconciliation has not yet come about. Nonetheless, a number of communities have gratefully made use of the possibilities provided by the Motu Proprio. On the other hand, difficulties remain concerning the use of the 1962 Missal outside of these groups, because of the lack of precise juridical norms, particularly because Bishops, in such cases, frequently feared that the authority of the Council would be called into question. Immediately after the Second Vatican Council it was presumed that requests for the use of the 1962 Missal would be limited to the older generation which had grown up with it, but in the meantime it has clearly been demonstrated that young persons too have discovered this liturgical form, felt its attraction, and found in it a form of encounter with the Mystery of the Most Holy Eucharist particularly suited to them. Thus the need has arisen for a clearer juridical regulation which had not been foreseen at the time of the 1988 Motu Proprio. The present norms are also meant to free Bishops from constantly having to evaluate anew how they are to respond to various situations.

In the second place, the fear was expressed in discussions about the awaited Motu Proprio, that the possibility of a wider use of the 1962 Missal would lead to disarray or even divisions within parish communities. This fear also strikes me as quite unfounded. The use of the old Missal presupposes a certain degree of liturgical formation and some knowledge of the Latin language; neither of these is found very often. Already from these concrete presuppositions, it is clearly seen that the new Missal will certainly remain the ordinary Form of the Roman Rite, not only on account of the juridical norms, but also because of the actual situation of the communities of the faithful.

It is true that there have been exaggerations and at times social aspects unduly linked to the attitude of the faithful attached to the ancient Latin liturgical tradition. Your charity and pastoral prudence will be an incentive and guide for improving these. For that matter, the two Forms of the usage of the Roman Rite can be mutually enriching: new Saints and some of the new Prefaces can and should be inserted in the old Missal. The *"Ecclesia Dei"* Commission, in contact with various bodies devoted to the *usus antiquior*, will study the practical possibilities in this regard. The celebration of the Mass according to the Missal of Paul VI will be able to demonstrate, more powerfully than has been the case hitherto, the sacrality which attracts many people to the former usage. The most sure guarantee that the Missal of Paul VI can unite parish communities and be loved by them consists in its being celebrated with great reverence in harmony with the liturgical directives. This will bring out the spiritual richness and the theological depth of this Missal.

I now come to the positive reason which motivated my decision to issue this Motu Proprio updating that of 1988. It is a matter of coming to an interior reconciliation in the heart of the Church. Looking back over the past, to the divisions which in the course of the centuries have rent the Body of Christ, one continually has the impression that, at critical moments when divisions were coming about, not enough was done by the Church's leaders to maintain or regain reconciliation and unity. One has the impression that omissions on the part of the Church have had their share of blame for the fact that these divisions were able to harden. This glance at the past imposes an obligation on us today: to make every effort to enable for all those who truly desire unity to remain in that unity or to attain it anew. I think of a sentence in the Second Letter to the Corinthians, where Paul writes: "Our mouth is open to you, Corinthians; our heart is wide. You are not restricted by us, but you are restricted in your own affections. In return . . . widen your hearts also!" (*2 Cor* 6:11–13). Paul was certainly speaking in another context, but his exhortation can and must touch us too, precisely on this subject. Let us generously open our hearts and make room for everything that the faith itself allows.

There is no contradiction between the two editions of the Roman Missal. In the history of the liturgy there is growth and progress, but no rupture. What earlier generations held as sacred remains sacred and great for us too, and it cannot be all of a sudden entirely forbidden or even considered harmful. It behooves all of us to preserve the riches which have developed in the Church's faith and prayer and to give them their proper place. Needless to say, in order to experience full communion, the priests of the communities adhering to the former usage cannot, as a matter of principle, exclude celebrating according to the new books. The total exclusion of the new rite would not in fact be consistent with the recognition of its value and holiness.

In conclusion, dear Brothers, I very much wish to stress that these new norms do not in any way lessen your own authority and responsibility, either for the liturgy or for the pastoral care of your faithful. Each Bishop, in fact, is the moderator of the liturgy in his own Diocese (cf. *Sacrosanctum Concilium*, 22: "Sacrae Liturgiae moderatio ab Ecclesiae auctoritate unice pendet quae quidem est apud Apostolicam Sedem et, ad normam iuris, apud Episcopum").

Nothing is taken away, then, from the authority of the Bishop, whose role remains that of being watchful that all is done in peace and serenity. Should some problem arise which the parish priest cannot resolve, the local Ordinary will always be able to intervene, in full harmony, however, with all that has been laid down by the new norms of the Motu Proprio.

Furthermore, I invite you, dear Brothers, to send to the Holy See an account of your experiences three years after this Motu Proprio has taken effect. If truly serious difficulties come to light, ways to remedy them can be sought.

Dear Brothers, with gratitude and trust, I entrust to your hearts as Pastors these pages and the norms of the Motu Proprio. Let us always be mindful of the words of the Apostle Paul addressed to the presbyters of Ephesus: "Take heed to yourselves and to all the flock, in which the Holy Spirit has made you overseers, to care for the Church of God which he obtained with the blood of his own Son" (*Acts* 20:28).

I entrust these norms to the powerful intercession of Mary, Mother of the Church, and I cordially impart my Apostolic Blessing to you, dear Brothers, to the parish priests of your dioceses, and to all the priests, your co-workers, as well as to all your faithful.

Given at Saint Peter's, 7 July 2007

BENEDICTUS PP. XVI

A SHORT BIBLIOGRAPHY

To Arrive at a Correct Idea of the Roman Liturgy

I.

Benedict XVI. Address to the Roman Curia. December 22, 2005.

———. Apostolic letter in the form of motu proprio *Summorum Pontificum*. July 7, 2007.

Catechism of the Catholic Church. 2nd ed. Vatican City: Libreria Editrice Vaticana; Washington, D.C.: United States Catholic Conference, 1997. §§ 1066–1209.

Compendium: Catechism of the Catholic Church. Vatican City: Libreria Editrice Vaticana; Washington, D.C.: United States Conference of Catholic Bishops, 2006. §§ 218–249.

Congregation for Sacred Worship and the Discipline of the Sacraments. Instruction *Redemptionis Sacramentum.* March 25, 2004.

John Paul II. Chirograph for the Centenary of the Motu Proprio *Tra le Sollecitudini*. December 3, 2003.

———. Encyclical letter *Ecclesia de Eucharistia.* April 17, 2003.

This is far from being an exhaustive bibliography: these are just a few titles chosen as providing a sound basic education in liturgy.

Second Vatican Council. Constitution on the Sacred Liturgy *Sacrosanctum Concilium*. December 4, 1963.

II. Introduction

Chalufour, Jean-Denis. *La Sainte Messe, hier, aujourd'hui et demain*. Petrus a Stella, 2000.

Gitton, Michel. *Initiation à la liturgie romaine*. Geneva: Ad Solem, 2003.

Gutierrez, José Luis. *Liturgie—Manuel d'initiation*. Madrid: Le Laurier, 2007.

III. More Depth and Detail

Bouyer, Louis. *Liturgy and Architecture*. Notre Dame, Ind.: Univ. of Notre Dame Press, 1967.

———. *Eucharist: Theology and Spirituality of the Eucharistic Prayer*. Translated by Charles Underhill Quinn. Univ. of Notre Dame Press, 1968.

Lang, U. M. *Turning towards the Lord: Orientation in Liturgical Prayer*. San Francisco: Ignatius Press, 2004.

Nichols, Aidan. *Looking at the Liturgy: A Critical View of Its Contemporary Form*. San Francisco: Ignatius Press, 1996.

Ratzinger, Joseph Cardinal. *The Feast of Faith*. Translated by Graham Harrison. San Francisco: Ignatius Press, 1986.

———. *A New Song for the Lord: Faith in Christ and Liturgy Today*. Translated by Martha M. Matesich. New York: Crossroad, 1997.

———. *The Spirit of the Liturgy*. Translated by John Saward. San Francisco: Ignatius Press, 2000.

IV. Various

Cassingena-Trévedy, François. *Te Igitur: Le Missel de saint Pie V*. Geneva: Ad Solem, 2007.

Crouan, Denis. *The Liturgy after Vatican II: Collapsing or Resurgent?* Translated by Mark Sebanc. San Francisco: Ignatius Press, 2001.

Esquier, Geneviève. *La Liturgie selon Vatican II*. Paris: F.-X. de Guibert, 2003.

Gamber, Klaus. *The Reform of the Roman Liturgy: Its Problems and Background*. Translated by Klaus D. Grimm. San Juan Capistrano, Calif.: Una Voce Press; Harrison, N.Y.: Foundation for Catholic Reform: 1993.

INDEX